The Elijah Awakening

CALLING DOWN THE FIRE IN AMERICA

Elijah's Miracles & the Jezebel Agenda

THE WHIRLWIND IS COMING

DONALD A. MOSS

The Elijah Awakening

Calling Down the Fire in America
Elijah's Miracles & the Jezebel Agenda
All Rights Reserved © 2021 by Donald A. Moss

Elijah Awakening Press

For information:
www.elijahawakening.com

This product provides information with regard to the subject matter covered. While a great deal of care has been taken to provide accurate information, the ideas, suggestions, general principles and conclusions presented in this text are not guaranteed and are subject to the personal experiences of the reader. Every situation is unique and the reader will determine the results obtained from use of this material.

This product is not intended to replace the professional services of a counselor, physician, minister, or any other such assistance. This product is not intended to offer legal advice, promise any mental, physical, or other benefit. Further, it is not intended to promote illegality, insurrection, vigilantism, revolution, or any other action outside the boundaries of the law.

ISBN: 978-1-7376984-0-1 (paperback)
ISBN: 978-1-7376984-1-8 (digital)

Printed in the United States of America.

CONTENTS

INTRODUCTION

One day in ancient Israel, a rugged prophet of God called Elijah, walked alone, out of the mountains, and into a royal palace to challenge wicked rulers and their abominable religion that reveled in nature worship, sexual perversity and child sacrifice. Mind-boggling explosions of heavenly fire and bloody confrontations would soon follow, to prove the power of Almighty God. It was the only solution to Israel's terrible problem.

Now, America is in need of a similar, heavenly solution. This book seeks to encapsulate a prophetic revelation of the "God solution" that is about to happen in America – an explosion of Truth that will revolutionize Christian believers. Patriots who love God need to be encouraged. We need to take heart and *know* the Truth that makes us free and stop listening to the lunatic Left, blow-dried, spinmeister, fake news types, trying to convince us of their Godless, alternate reality.

So, in the spirit of Elijah, this book seeks to fore-warn of an approaching revival of Holy Ghost power soon to explode in America and set off a spiritual revolution against the kingdom of darkness. *That* is God's solution to America's current devil problem. Indeed, it is the *spiritual dimension* of American life that holds the key to our future.

In these pages, we will unmask the enemy – the evil Jezebel Agenda – and discover what God is saying about the *Elijah Awakening*. We will unveil how the Old Testament miracles of Elijah may be spiritually discerned and actual-ized in the fight against the evil that has a chokehold on America today. We will discover the military-like hierarchies of Satan's dark kingdom and how God used two important prophets (Elijah and Daniel) to deal with such unspeakable evil. In the final analysis, this work is about God-ordained men and women in America, speaking Truth to power, in a supernatural confrontation with the kingdom of darkness, just like Elijah did in ancient Israel.

Based on a powerful visitation by the Lord and a fresh revelation of the Scriptures (check out the *Afterword*), I believe ordinary American Christians will soon be arrayed on the front lines of spiritual combat. The Holy Spirit will empower them to leave their sanctuaries and step onto the battlefield as anointed gladiators to confront the ene-mies of God. I glimpsed some of this several years ago as a nation-shaking move of the Holy Spirit. (Donald A. Moss, *The Third Day: A Revelation of the Coming Revival,* Writers Club Press 2002). We need to get ready.

Already, some American pastors are seeing the initial droplets of this latter rain that will be unlike anything we have seen before. Across the nation, here and there, believers are reporting a change in the winds of God. (God uses the winds to gather His people together.) In this, I believe God will use the coming revival to unify and transform the Body of Christ into the **Army of God** assigned to confront evil in the land, wage war on the kingdom of darkness and prepare people for the return of Jesus. Church leadership will be electrified and redefined to prepare them for a type of supernatural battle we have never seen before. Not to worry, the Holy Spirit will provide what is needed.

The lost will flood America's sanctuaries to be saved and miracles will confirm the Word of the Lord. Even the smallest country church will suddenly fill to standing room only with people starving for the life-changing power of God. This revival will not be an isolated event in some small corner of the country. Instead, it will happen everywhere at once, like lightning flashing from east to west.

Tragically, America has been assaulted like a wounded antelope torn apart and pulled down by ravening wolves. Much of this is the work of dark forces to bring about a globalist lie known as the "Great Reset." But it is far more sinister than just a "reset." It is a demonic "Great Manipulation," that is now being pushed aggressively by globalist elites, to enslave mankind. The main thrust of the Great Reset is to remove the individual freedoms and liberties of the working class, and replace them with the ideals and wisdom of the all-knowing elite. This is a hellish agenda and it guarantees the destruction of America as founded.

But there is more to this than meets the eye.

Each year, movers and shakers from across the globe gather together at the annual World Economic Forum in Davos, a posh ski resort in the Swiss Alps. Attendance is invitation-only and enforced by police barricades and razor wire. Global problems are defined and discussed by those who hold the greatest concentrations of wealth.

Davos is, in essence, a political network – ergo the "Party of Davos" – that rules the global market in hopeful preparation for a *one world government* (think: the government of the Antichrist). Americans play a big role in this effort because the Party of Davos, relies on the resources of the US superpower to support its agenda. In exchange, the American members of the Party of Davos receive special treatment. Thus, the global economy is developing a global ruling class and an evil system which only protects one class of global citizen – the corporate investor. Its greatest threat is the America First, populist nationalism agenda of Donald J. Trump, also known as "Trumpism."

"Make America Great Again" (MAGA) is the political war cry of freedom-loving Americans of every race who believe in God, life, liberty and justice for all – America's founding principles. It includes brave notions of populist nationalism, "America First" priorities, vilified by the establishment elites (i.e., fake news media, entertainment industry, liberal universities, so-called intellectuals and the scoffing punditry). MAGA is about the *aristocracy of the common man*, NOT globalist ruling elites or the Washington swamp (the Uniparty). America is the land of the free and home of the brave. Our forefathers fought and died in wars around the globe for this powerful notion.

MAGA became the grand slogan and rallying cry for supporters of Donald J. Trump, the 45th President of the United States seen on red ball caps and signs and flags nationwide. MAGA identifies decent, God-fearing lovers of faith, freedom and family. Hillary Clinton disdainfully called us "Deplorables." Joe Biden imperiously denigrated us as "Neanderthal thinkers." Whatever. There are millions of us and we are tired of being bullied and dismissed.

Amid the confusion of a Coronavirus pandemic causing nationwide lockdowns and wreaking havoc on the US economy, explosive allegations of November 3, 2020 election fraud came forth. Rallies were held, monies were raised. Emotions ran high in the nation. Time and again the justice system (including SCOTUS) failed the American people and cases were tossed (avoided at all costs) for outlandish reasons of "lack of proper standing" or "laches." Then, to the dismay of millions of Trump supporters, the feckless Joe Biden was installed (by the "drive-by" corporate media) as the 46th President of the United States. Now, according to some post-election polls, large percentages of Americans believe the 2020 presidential election was stolen from the incumbent President Donald J. Trump by egregious acts of fraud in several key states. It should be noted that Biden arrogantly bragged, "*We have put together, I think, the most extensive and inclusive voter fraud organization in the history of American politics.*"[1] If true, such criminal behavior is beyond the pale and impossible for the American people to accept.

Biden, the flawed candidate who hid in his basement and could not draw a crowd, was inaugurated on January 20, 2021, despite great legal efforts to stop the alleged steal. Something went horribly wrong. Among the many great legal minds involved in challenges to the alleged sham election, former Assistant US. Attorney and "Super Lawyer," the great Sidney Powell, was quoted as saying, "*...from my perspective it looks like the complete breakdown of every insti-*

tution of law enforcement and the rule of law that we have trusted in this country since its inception to protect the law and the citizens from abuses by the government."2

Based on the tragic events of an alleged "insurrection" by Trump supporters on January 6th (infiltrated by undercover radicals posing as MAGA), the US Capitol became an armed camp barricaded by razor-wire and thousands of National Guard troops. It remained a militarized zone to keep Americans away from the political class in Washington, DC, much like third world dictatorships around the world. Vengeful congressional House Democrats ran amok and impeached (but did not convict in the Senate) President Donald Trump, not once, but twice. The second impeachment in 2021, based on Trump's alleged role in the so-called "insurrection," was little more than a thinly veiled, but failed attempt by panicked Democrats to prevent him from running for office again.

This sustained insanity has only one real explanation: the radical Left has crossed the Rubicon and America has fallen under the spell of unseen powers, principalities and rulers of the darkness on the earth.

Please understand that Satan is not in hell. John the Revelator wrote, *"The great dragon was hurled down—that ancient serpent called the devil, or Satan, who leads the whole world astray. He was hurled to the earth, and his angels with him.* "3 He moves around from place to place on the earth and in the second heaven. Lucifer admitted that he kept busy, *"...from going to and fro in the earth, and from walking up and down in it."*4 However, he does more than just walk around. The apostle Peter observed, *"Be sober, be vigilant; because your adversary the devil, as a roaring lion, walketh about, seeking whom he may devour."*5 Like a wild lion, he will devour those ignorant enough to get too close.

Satan has always obsessed over political power. Because of his rebellion against God, he was cast down to the earth and found his place in American politics. His fingerprints are all over the Godless insanity espoused by the radical, Marxist Left ignorantly cheering on the globalist order that will pave the way for the rise of the murderous Antichrist and his one world government. In a nutshell, Satan has beguiled many Americans who now believe our rights as Americans must flow from an all-powerful government, not God, and that government can change our rights at its whim.

This ideology favors killing unborn humans, but demands prison time for anyone who mistreats animals. It denies the scientific and Scriptural fact that life begins at conception. Radical adherents want to kill the elderly because they are a burden to a progressive society. They believe illegal aliens should be counted with American citizens when apportioning congressional House seats and allowed to vote. This explains why they want open borders. They want to give the right to vote to convicted felons. They deny the science that there are two sexes and that sex is determined by DNA. They promote the hatred of the police, the defunding of police and the insanity that cops must be utterly perfect or face imprisonment. They want to destroy the 2nd Amendment, ban guns, disarm law-abiding citizens and allow armed criminals to rule the streets. They want to destroy all things Trump and deem MAGA patriots as "domestic terrorists." According to leftists, the American flag is racist, the National Anthem is offensive and the term "patriot" is hate speech. There is no end in sight to the insanity and the vitriol. It seems these radicals on the Left are out for blood!

However, a big surprise is coming for them all. They will lose this war because Satan does not have the power and authority to destroy those who follow Christ. Jesus said, *"I saw Satan fall like lightning from heaven. Behold, I have given you authority to trample on snakes and scorpions and to overcome all the power of the enemy; nothing will harm you."*[6]

Alas, Satan can only destroy the fools who give him place.

Betrayal is the devil's dagger. Satan will eventually eviscerate the very people who pledge allegiance to him. Those who have been blinded by his lies will be horrified and they will panic. The enemies of God will be scattered. They will flee, but no way of escape will be found. *"It will be as though a man fled from a lion only to meet a bear, as though he entered his house and rested his hand on the wall only to have a snake bite him."*7 Only the Truth provides us the power to walk through the valley of death and fear no evil.

The agenda of God prevails yesterday, today and forever. As the Apostle Paul stated to the church at Ephesus, our struggle is not against flesh and blood, but against evil forces in the supernatural realm. As citizens of the heavenly kingdom through Jesus Christ, believers have a dominion birthright over the earth. We love freedom because we love God! Where the Spirit of the Lord is, there is liberty and America is not lost yet. What is about to happen next will set things in spiritual order and breathe freedom into our souls again.

Nothing can stop what God is about to do. The high fences and razor wire displayed in the nation's capitol do not affect Almighty God. The paranoia of the powerful will not stop the One who commands the winds and walks on water. America haters of every color and stripe will be as chaff blown in a whirlwind when God claps His hands and releases the mighty hosts of heaven from sea to shining sea. This great spiritual awakening is coming to America and there is no force in the universe to stop it. The key to this event lies within the pages of Scripture involving the spirit of Elijah and the return of Christ.

Jesus alluded to His second coming with a comment about Elijah, *"Elijah truly will come first and restore all things."*8 Taken literally, it means that Elijah will reappear in person during the Tribulation period and before Christ returns. Taken another way, the Elijah anointing will be a defining *characteristic* of a spiritual revival that will lead God's army to confront evil in high places to destroy the works of the devil and restore America's relationship with God. It will prepare the way for Jesus' return. It will set men free. *"Where the Spirit of the Lord is, there is liberty."*9 The *Elijah Awakening* is a "present day" manifestation or glimpse of Jesus' prophecy of the tribulation period, that will help restore liberty in America, by confronting workers of iniquity in the kingdom of darkness.

The Scriptures in the Book of Daniel, Chapter 11, detail earthly events, but are also a glimpse beyond the veil of evil dark rulers who corrupt with smooth words those who hate the things of God and coerce them into the satanic dark kingdom. In Chapter 10, a heavenly angel sent to help Daniel was attacked by a powerful demon or dark ruler that was *assigned to influence* the human King of Persia. It appears that our government and judicial systems are now brimming with the madness of these unclean spirits, intent on defiling the very fabric of America. However, we have a powerful promise that the people who know their God shall be strong and do great exploits, in spite of the devil.10 We should take heart. A whirlwind of God's restoring power will soon hit America like a hurricane.

Now watch this.

Spiritual revival begins and flourishes when the power of the devil is confronted by the Word of God. The head of the serpent is crushed under the feet of the revived Church. This Truth will turn a lost world upside down and set captives free. Where the Spirit of the Lord is, there is liberty and justice for all! The Scriptures declare that the very reason the Son of God appeared was to destroy the works of the devil who came to steal, kill and destroy. True revival is all about the recognition and confrontation of sin, subsequent repentance and God's wonderful forgiveness which restores our relationship with God. In this way, MAGA explodes with new meaning – Make America God's Again – because America is God's country.

And so, we are brought to the explosive subject matter of this book. The spiritual American warrior giant will rise in *The Elijah Awakening* to confront evil and deliver the thunderous Word of the Lord to prepare the way for His return. Nothing will be able to separate us from the love of God in this hour.

And nothing will be able to stop us from the call of God to rescue our land.

CHAPTER ONE

The Jezebel Agenda

"...but he (Ahab) also married Jezebel daughter of Ethbaal king of the Sidonians, and began to serve Baal and worship him." 1 Kings 16:31 KJV

"...My people have exchanged their glorious God for worthless idols. Be appalled at this, you heavens, and shudder with great horror," declares the LORD. My people have committed two sins: they have forsaken me, the spring of living water, and have dug their own cisterns, broken cisterns that cannot hold water" Jeremiah 2:11-13 KJV.

J ezebel's terrible agenda in America provides a diabolical mechanism by which evil power is released from the kingdom of darkness into the earthly realm. It serves Satan's master plan which is to steal, kill and destroy in America by luring people away from God with a drastic, cultural transformation. This wicked program has nothing to do with targeting or degrading the female gender. It does have both natural and supernatural aspects largely unrecognized by most Americans consumed with the everyday distractions of life. But this enemy exists nonetheless and the "Jezebel Agenda" is aptly named because it is inextricably tied to the hellish spirituality of an evil personality from the distant past.

The historical Jezebel left a terrible legacy of demon worship, sexual deviancy, murder, revenge and cruelty. She promoted a murderous purge of the prophets and the worship of Jehovah in ancient Israel. In short, she challenged Almighty God and lost.

Jezebel was Torn Apart by Dogs

God deals harshly with rebellion. In the dateless past, Lucifer was cast out of God's heaven (along with one-third of the angelic host) for leading a treasonous rebellion against God. At her bloody end, Jezebel was cast out of a high window to be torn and eaten by feral dogs in the street. But human souls are the devil's prize and powers, principalities and rulers of darkness never rest in their quest to ruin the unsuspecting.

The Scriptures declare, *"...where the Spirit of the Lord is, there is liberty."*1 Freedom lives where the Holy Spirit is given place. But when the Jezebel spirit takes control to purge God from the nation and beguile those who will bend the knee to abomination and blasphemy, the kingdom of darkness quickly establishes an evil throne and installs a dark ruler to sit upon it. This is the supernatural drama currently being played out in a radically transformed America.

America Transformed into an anti-God Hellhole

Sleepy Joe Biden and his "woke" masters yearn to fundamentally transform America into an anti-God, hellhole. The scheming for this cultural transformation began in earnest long before the alleged stolen elections and Marxist fever dreams of installing an easily manipulated puppet were entertained. Now, the goal of the radical Left is to hold onto the ruling power they have taken and continue ripping the guts out of America as founded. Some try to soften the sound of their radical agenda by calling it, "democratic socialism." Pure democracy, without the rule of law, is nothing more than *mob rule*. Marxists often refer to socialism as the first, necessary phase on the way from capitalism to communism. They refer to communism as "revolutionary socialism." Trained Marxists believe that violent revolution is an inevitable part of achieving power.

Thus, the radical Left's playbook instructs enthusiasts to demoralize, destabilize and normalize the abnormal. The precepts of Christ must be purged from the landscape. But sin, like water, seeks its own level. This results in crooked rivers and crooked men. Foolish men. However, when foolish men forsake God's springs of living water and dig their own broken cisterns, bad things happen.

Biden and the Alien Invasion

American patriots are living in dangerous times. The Biden regime has thrown open our southern borders encouraging an invasion into America by multitudes of illegal immigrants from all over the world. This dangerous lunacy allows Mexican drug cartels to control the border and make *billions* in the human (child) trafficking business. Never mind American border towns turned into hot zones for rape and murder. Never mind the smorgasbord of diseases brought across causing border town hospitals to overflow with Covid cases. Biden and the wild hyenas supporting him have purposely orchestrated this chaos. Further, wide-eyed Democratic operatives giggle and salivate over the possibilities to transform these illegals into loyal Democrat voters *forever.* More of this alien invasion will be mentioned in another chapter.

What God Condemns, the Biden Regime Celebrates

The hard-line persecution of those who love God is imminent. American believers have never suffered for the cause of Christ like others have across the globe. But the hordes of hell are coming for us too. The government of the United States seems weaponized against God and devils are coming for our Bibles, our babies, our oil, our jobs and our guns. No one is safe. Today, if God's Word condemns it, the Biden regime celebrates it! Isaiah warned, *"Woe to those who call evil good and good evil, who put darkness for light and light for darkness, who put bitter for sweet and sweet for bitter."*2

In this madness, Americans still have access to the superior knowledge that God's truth provides. There are churches and Bible preachers across the country and thank God for them all. And the good news is that real Americans will win this fight against evil because God will fight for us.

But the fact remains that we can no longer sit at our ease when a supernatural war rages at our doorstep. Moreover, a terrible price will be paid because people always suffer and perish when God's truth and knowledge is rejected. Sadly, nations are utterly destroyed because of it.

Ancient Israel was Destroyed by Baalism

Ancient Israel was destroyed over time because they turned away from Jehovah and served their own lusts. In God's covenant with Abraham, Israel was promised blessings as God's chosen people and through them, all the nations would be blessed as long as they served God.3 During Israel's history, when the worship of Jehovah God prevailed, the people were blessed. The Bible declares, *"Blessed is the nation whose God is the LORD."*4

When Israel entered the Promised Land of Canaan under Joshua, they enjoyed a wonderful spiritual foundation with Jehovah. God instructed them to *"have no other gods before Me."*5 They were obedient to God and He took care of them. Prior to Joshua, under Moses, Israel learned some hard lessons about captivity in Egypt. But God delivered them from Egyptian bondage and set them free. He even parted the waters of the Red Sea to allow their escape from Pharaoh's army. Israel knew God was good because they were living witnesses to His grace. But when they entered the Promised Land, the natives of Canaan did not know Jehovah. They served the "Baals."

Dark Rulers Sit Upon Corrupt Thrones

The Hebrew word *Baal* means "lord" or "master." Baalzebub is also another name for Satan. In Canaan, the Baals were represented in various idols, but hidden behind the idols was something far more insidious – a demonic ruler sitting upon a throne as part of the hierarchy in Satan's kingdom of darkness. This occurs when people are seduced into giving a demonic ruler "place" or the right to rule. In this, a "corrupt throne" is then created and the evil power flows from it. The Apostle Paul declared, *"Neither give place to the devil."*6 The Psalmist asked, *"Can a corrupt throne be allied with you – a throne that brings on misery by its decrees?"*7

God knew all about this evil lurking in Canaan's shadows and sought to protect His chosen people from it. This explains why God commanded Israel to drive out the evil Canaanites and destroy their worship of Baal. Like cancer, sin must be removed or it will kill you. Sadly, Israel failed to obey God's directives and did not complete this assignment. Instead, they decided to *tolerate* instead of *eliminate* and things got worse.

Over time, Israel developed an insatiable lust for the pagan nature worship of their Canaanite neighbors. This was in direct violation of Mosaic Law which commanded Israel to refrain from worshiping false gods or nature. In the Ten Commandments, God gave Israel directives to love God, love parents and love others. But Israel was mesmerized and ignored God. Sadly, apostasy thrives when evil is tolerated. Evil triumphs when good men drink the poison "Kool-aid." Israel ignored Jehovah's commandments and drank the poison of "Baalism."

Sexual Perversity, Human Sacrifice and Jezebel

Baalism flooded the culture of Israel when its weak King Ahab was manipulated by his heathen wife, Jezebel, to introduce and promote the worship of the Tyrian god Baal-Melkart, a fertility or nature god. To do this, Jezebel had to destroy the exclusive worship of Jehovah throughout the land and replace it with a demon-inspired religion that featured sexual perversity and human sacrifice. Anyone who opposed wicked Jezebel was murdered for their trouble.

According to the historical record, Jezebel was the daughter of Ethbaal, the king of Tyre and Sidon. Ethbaal, a priest of Baal, had risen to power by murdering the king (his own brother) and stealing his throne. It is significant that her father was both pagan priest and king – a deadly blending of false religion and political authority that Jezebel would later try to recreate in her efforts to polarize public opinion against the prophets of Jehovah God. It is believed by some that the mother of Jezebel was also a high priestess of Baal.

Jezebel was the original Lady Macbeth. She was conniving and manipulative. She was the power behind the throne. The name Jezebel means "without cohabitation." Though she was wedded to the king of Israel, the union of Jezebel and the gullible Ahab was nothing more than a political alliance designed to harmonize the interests of Israel with the heathen nations of Tyre and Sidon. It is noteworthy that God's reaction to evil Ahab was rage.8 Almost immediately after the marriage, Jezebel, seizing on the weakness of her husband's corrupt character, began to exert tremendous influence in the affairs of Israel. To quickly spread the poison of Baalism, Jezebel sponsored 850 false prophets – 450 for Baal and 400 for Asherah, a goddess consort of Baal.9 In this, Jezebel magnified her power agenda and the opiate of Baalism was the perfect lure.

Baalism has a Pornographic Worship Scheme

Baalism indulges sex and promises wealth, health and pleasure. In ancient Israel, it blended sexual fertility and the desire for a corresponding agricultural fertility in a pornographic worship scheme that corrupted the entire nation. It produced wild promiscuity among the people of Israel and Judah.

The prophet Jeremiah declared to the kingdom of Judah, *"...Indeed, on every high hill and under every spreading tree you lay down as a prostitute."*10 He also compared Judah to a *"wild donkey"* and available *"at mating time"* for all the males who seek her.11 The Old Testament prophets viewed it as spiritual adultery and that Israel had broken her "marriage vows" with the Mosaic Covenant.

Babies were Murdered as Human Sacrifices

Thus, Baalism promoted sexual lust and encouraged promiscuity. Orgies and perversions of every kind were indulged. Unwanted babies were created from the orgies. Then, to gain favor with the pagan gods, they murdered these babies by throwing them alive into a fire pit to be burned to death. The Scriptures declare, *"Who inflame yourselves [with lust in pagan rites] among the oaks, under* *every green and leafy tree, Who slaughter the children [in sacrifice]…"*12

Baalism slowly consumed the entire country and corrupted its religious, political and business institutions and finally drained God's people dry. It strangled the ragged remains of the Mosaic Covenant and choked off the blessings of the promised land, leaving the country economically devastated. Thus, the Northern Kingdom of Israel began with freedom under the rule of God's law, but slid down into the quagmire of mysticism and child sacrifice. It collapsed under conspiracies and military coups, and finally ended in 722 BC with the Assyrian invasion and exile.13 They became known as the "lost 10 tribes of Israel." The Southern Kingdom of Judah ended in child sacrifice and the horrors of cannibalism14 during the Babylonian invasion in 586 BC.

During the time of Jezebel, demonic rituals involved idols of wood and stone that represented the ideas and entities behind Baal worship. Today, people do not need physical idols. They simply worship ideas. Radical ideas. "Woke" ideas.

Baalism is Disguised in America

In America, Baalism is disguised in demands for "sexual rights" and the insanity of "sexual orientation and gender identity." If John F. Kennedy put a man on the moon, then Joe Biden has put a man in the women's restroom. Biden picked a transgender person for assistant secretary of health. Biden also urged Congress to pass the "Equality Act," a bill that would eliminate any legal recognition of male and female sex, cater to gender ideology and designate protection for the unborn as "pregnancy discrimination." It would create a civil right for men *who identify as women* to enter the women's restroom, spend the night in a battered women's shelter, disrobe in a women's locker room and compete on a women's sports team—even children at K-12 public schools. The buried lead is that killing unborn children is tantamount to a civil right.

Abortion is Child Sacrifice in the Supernatural Realm

In Sleepy Joe's radicalized America, sexual rights and a culture of easy promiscuity produces unwanted babies. Then, the babies are aborted and their tiny bodies are incinerated or passed "...*through the fire to Molech.*"15 The act of abortion in the earthly realm becomes, in the supernatural realm, *child sacrifice*. The incineration of the bodies becomes, in the realm of devils, *burnt offerings*. It makes no difference to demons and higher echelon rulers of darkness whether sexually liberated Americans have ever heard of Baal or the fires of Molech or ancient Canaan, for that matter.

As faith attracts God, so does sin attract devils. The kingdom of darkness views America's abortions and fiery disposal methods as the spiritual equivalent to sacrificing and passing children through the fire in ancient Israel. In both cases, the demons rejoice.

Aborted Babies are the Food Source for Demonic Rulers

This horror is of paramount importance to God-loving patriots in America. Why? Aborted children are *the primary food source* (read: considered *worship* by devils) for the ruling demonic entities. When children are sacrificed (aborted), the lusts of the demonic ruler are temporarily appeased, resulting in a release of dark power or diabolical influence or favor from its corrupt throne of iniquity into the realm of humanity. This release of evil power energizes carnal tendencies in humans stirring lusts to commit certain sins and the process begins again. But this is a Faustian bargain and people are unwittingly lured deeper into jeopardy and farther away from God. It is likely the primary reason God was so provoked to rage by Ahab and Jezebel was the act of harming children, the literal future of Israel.

Children are very important to God. Jesus said, *"It would be better for him if a millstone were hung around his neck, and he were thrown into the sea, than that he should offend one of these little ones."*16 If killing and incinerating babies in ancient Israel provoked God to hot anger, what will become of the radical Left's America?

Today, there are two kinds of Americans. There are Americans who love Jesus Christ and the infallible Word of God. They love the nation of Israel and pray for the peace of Jerusalem. They are patriots who cherish the Constitution and freedom. Then, there are those who are in service to something else. Jesus drove this point home by declaring, *"Whoever is not with me is against me, and whoever does not gather with me scatters."*17

Today, there is much scattering in America.

The Jezebel Agenda

1. Control the King to Control the People.

"There was never anyone like Ahab, who sold himself to do evil in the eyes of the Lord, <u>urged on by Jezebel</u> his wife." (1 Kings 21:25 NIV).

- Gain power behind the throne by means of a weak leader.
- Exercise power by connivance and manipulation of weak leadership.
- Control power by intimidation, manipulation and domination of others.
- Prioritize power and politics over people.
- Control healthcare.
- Control education.
- Control guns.
- Control speech.
- Control food supply.
- Control housing.
- Control income.

2. **Purge Jehovah and His prophets.**

"While Jezebel was killing off the Lord's prophets..." (1 Kings 18:4 NIV).

- Remove God from government and schools.
- Cancel Judeo-Christian culture using corporate and social media.
- Criminalize Judeo-Christian principles with evil laws.
- Crush churches and ministers using woke cancel culture, anti-God laws and public health edicts.
- Persecute the American church using US government agencies: IRS, FBI, DHS, DOJ and others.

3. **Recast Baalism as Nature Worship and Sexual Freedom.**

"Against whom do ye sport yourselves? Against whom make ye a wide mouth, and draw out the tongue? Are ye not children of transgression, a seed of falsehood, Enflaming yourselves with idols under every green tree, slaying the children in the valleys under the clifts of the rocks?" (Isaiah 57:4-5)*

- Recast the nature worship of Baalism into the religion of "Climate Change."
- Recast the sexuality of ancient Baalism into modern sexual liberation, abortion, gender identity, LGTBQ politics.
- Recast ancient child sacrifice into modern abortion and incineration disposal.

*Note: *Ancient Baalism combined nature worship, sexual abandon and child sacrifice into both outdoor settings and in the Temple of Baal. Now, as then, the activities of Baal worship produces a release of evil power from the throne of a demonic ruling entity into the region in its control. Demonic oppression and possession become more pronounced in this atmosphere.*

4. **Recruit the Poor.**

"I assure you that there were many widows in Israel in Elijah's time, when the sky was shut for three and a half years and there was a severe famine throughout the land." (Luke 4:25 NIV)*

- Increase class consciousness by destroying the middle class and dividing the people into rich and poor.
- Increase poverty through taxation.
- Increase reliance on government handouts to control those who are in poverty, disenfranchised, fearful, bitter and angry.
- Increase recruiting efforts through illegal immigration and open borders.

Note: *The reason Jezebel was successful in recruiting Israel to Baalism was based on poverty and economics... the rains brought by Baal caused the crops to grow and thus prosperity would ensue for the agricultural based society. It is possible that 1 million people lived in the Northern Kingdom of Israel during the reign of Ahab and Jezebel, but only a tiny minority of 7,000 still served Jehovah. The vast majority served Baal. The lure into Baalism was sexual deviancy and promises of relief from economic suffering.*

5. **Turn the hearts of the children away from the fathers** – *"See, I will send the prophet Elijah to you*

before that great and dreadful day of the LORD comes. He will turn the hearts of the parents to their children, and the hearts of the children to their parents; or else I will come and strike the land with total destruction." (Malachi 4:5-6)*

- Indoctrinate a new generation that will despise and demolish America's founding principles.
- Tear down the statues.
- Teach revisionist history.
- Diminish senior citizens to obliterate their moral wisdom and influence.
- Teach hatred and revolution.
- Disrespect law and order.
- Denigrate capitalistic values and American exceptionalism.

*Note: *If Elijah was sent to turn hearts back, then Baalism turned them away.*

CHAPTER TWO

The Elijah Awakening

"Behold, I will send you Elijah the prophet before the coming of the great and dreadful day of the Lord: And he will turn the hearts of the fathers to the children, and the hearts of the children to their fathers, lest I come and strike the earth with a curse." Malachi 4:5-6 KJV

"Jesus answered and said to them, "Indeed, Elijah is coming first and will restore all things." Matthew 17:11 KJV.

The *Elijah Awakening* is a wonderful spiritual transformation that will surely fall like the rain on God's people. Just as Jesus was raised on the third day, a powerful supernatural event is about to occur on the earth. From an obscure Old Testament prophecy found in Hosea 6:1-2, comes the shocking prediction of an explosion of heavenly power that will bring healing and revival in a time period identified in my previous book as the *Third Day.*

We are Now in the Third Day of Grace

In Bible terms, a day is as a thousand years. Two thousand years or two days of grace have elapsed since the death and resurrection of Jesus. The third day of grace or the third one thousand year period from the time of Christ will provide a time of finishing grace. Some call it the latter rain. It will be an awesome outpouring of the Spirit of God to prepare believers for the coming of Christ in the clouds. We are now living in the third day of grace. The spirit of the Old Testament prophet Elijah will greatly characterize the coming revival of the Third Day.

Elijah dominated Bible history for calling down fire from heaven and later, for being taken to heaven in a whirlwind with a chariot of fire and horses of fire. Fire flashes from the mouths of the two prophetic witnesses in Revelation 11, to destroy those who wish to harm them. One of those fiery witnesses will be Elijah.

Americans will Know When God
Anoints Them as Elijahs

Elijah and the fire of God go hand in hand. Elijah confronted an evil government and the apostasy of a nation. Elijah spoke and God sent fire. The fire of God burns away corruption and things we do not need. Fire purifies and refines. It can transform raw materials into beautiful works of art. It can melt things together to repair and make them stronger. Holy Ghost fire will produce the "Elijah" anointing in men and women transforming them into powerful firebrands for righteousness in the public arena. When it happens, *they will know who they are* by the anointing of the Holy Spirit and they will arise as warriors from every corner of the country. These patriots will confront evil just as Elijah the prophet once did. God will use the spiritual fire of the *Elijah Awakening* to destroy wickedness and restore America as one nation under God.

Malachi prophesied of the return of Elijah and stated that he will turn the hearts of the fathers and their children to each other. This does not refer to settling family disputes among Israelites. Its spiritual meaning goes much deeper and characterizes our ancestry and the Godly foundations created by our fathers – the founding fathers of our nation. We are the children of God and as patriotic Americans, we are also the descendant children of America's founding. As Christians, we are spiritual Israel, part of God's chosen people. These concepts flow one into the other. The *Elijah Awakening* will help restore the Godly principles of our founding fathers and God will restore America with the revival fire of the Holy Spirit.

Elijah is Coming to Restore

Then, Jesus also speaks of Elijah coming *to restore all things*.1 Some think Christ is referring *only* to John the Baptist. Peter, James and John thought so. But they had just seen Jesus transfigured on the mountain and talking with both Moses and Elijah. God spoke to them out of a cloud. Needless to say, the disciples were quite rattled, even afraid. As they walked down the mountain, Jesus told them not to tell anyone what they had just seen until after He was raised from the dead. This led to their question as to why it was written that Elijah must come first? The answer requires an open mind and some spiritual eyesight.

First, Jesus told them that Elijah would come first and restore all things and then, He stated that Elijah had already come. This likely confused Peter, James and John. Thus, the scriptures state the disciples understood Jesus to *only* mean John the Baptist. But there is more to this than simply the level of understanding of three awestruck men who had just seen Jesus' face shine like the sun, the miraculous appearance of Moses and Elijah talking with Him and then God speaking to them out of a cloud. The disciples were having trouble comprehending these wild events.

But, we must press on.

Based on His phrasing, it seems unlikely that Jesus was speaking of John the Baptist and nothing else. So, who else was He talking about? Christ was not speaking of *the* Elijah, but *an* Elijah. Indeed, Jesus was articulating a fresh revelation about a future messenger(s) coming in the *spirit* of Elijah. Thus, the spirit of Elijah will transform certain Americans to confront the agenda of Jezebel and bring the message of spiritual restoration in America.

The *Elijah Awakening* will prepare believers for the return of Christ. It will happen before the great and dreadful "Day of the Lord." This is a frightful, even enigmatic term that scholars have associated first with the crucifixion of Christ and then again, as the terrible, end-time events known as "the tribulation period" ahead of us in the future.

Powerful Men and Women Will be Forerunners

In context, John the Baptist was the forerunner to Jesus' ministry on earth, but the *Elijah Awakening* will produce powerful men and women of God who will be fore-runners to the end-time return of Christ. They will *restore* things. Restoration speaks to returning something of value that has been taken away. The "American way" has been stolen out from under God's people and we need a power-ful restoration to get back what the devil has taken.

This spiritual event will bring a potent mixture of faithfulness to God and fearless prophetic activism that will challenge the agenda of Jezebel (Baalism) in America. Make no mistake, we may hold to account the radical Left and the evil Washington swamp for ruining the nation, but the real source of America's troubles emanate from malevolent enemies within the supernatural kingdom of Satan. War must be declared on these agents of darkness. Supernatural accounts must be brought to balance. This explains why God is about to regenerate the Church with an explosion of miracle power and authority to accomplish His purposes.

The Body of Christ Transformed to the Army of God

Like lightning flashing across the horizon, the Church will be transformed from the Body of Christ into the war-time *Army of God.* Christian sunshine soldiers and sum-mer patriots will either move aside or be changed in the twinkling of an eye and filled with an "Elijah" anointing, empowering them like never before to confront evil in dark shadows. Signs and wonders will confirm the Word of the Lord, as modern day American prophets will obey the directives of God, to confront and destroy the works of a demonic system, much like the prophet Elijah did so long ago.

To gain greater understanding of this, we must travel back in time to ancient Israel in the 9th century BC. The Israelites, God's chosen people, foolishly divided themselves into two kingdoms consisting of the northern tribes (Israel) and southern tribes (Judah). However, Jehovah, the God of Abraham, Isaac and Jacob, was worshiped by the people of both kingdoms in the city of Jerusalem (southern kingdom). Over time, the Northern Kingdom of Israel and its kings sought religions that indulged and accentuated their growing depravities. So, they disobeyed God and strayed into the demonic practices of pagan worship which included the golden calf and the demon god, Baal. As a result, Jehovah was shoved aside.

False Prophets on Every Corner

Moreover, these evil monarchs sought to aggressively promote paganism by establishing heathen worship sites away from Jerusalem. For example, the altar and temple of Baal was built by evil King Ahab in Samaria, the capital city of Israel. In essence, the people were drawn into a treasonous disobedience to Jehovah through the evil policies of their own government. False prophets stood on every corner to promote the agenda of hell and encourage idolatry and wickedness.

An Ancient Game of Thrones

Conspiracies, betrayals and assassinations occurred in this ancient game of thrones, until King Ahab gained power. The scriptures declare he did more to provoke God to anger than all of the kings of Israel before him.2 What evil acts could possibly enrage God so much? The answer has a direct relationship to the evil in America today and reveals something important about the nature of God. This particular and insidious evil can be called the "Jezebel Agenda," because its tenets involve human sacrifice and blasphemy and such wickedness always provokes God.

When God Sends an Elijah to Declare War

When God is provoked to great anger, He sends prophets to declare war and judgment. He sends the fire. God sends an Elijah.

Elijah the Tishbite came forth out of the wilderness of the sparsely populated Gilead. The people of this rocky hill country were rough, rugged and stern of character. They were shepherds and lived close to the land in crude dwellings rather than lavish palaces. He was called "Tishbite" probably after Tishbe, an area in Gilead, as supposed by the Jewish historian Josephus. Tishbite means, "inhabitants," or "strangers." Elijah was a stranger borne out of a wilderness. Today, he would likely be dismissed as one of Hillary Clinton's "deplorables." But, the "better than thou" attitudes of sore losers such as Hillary and her ilk have no place in the prophetic realm.

Elijah was a Rugged Mountain Man

Elijah stood in striking contrast to the effeminate and perverted priests of Baal wearing gowns of fine, white linen and eating palace delicacies. He certainly did not fit in with the rich folks living in the capital city. His dress and appearance, the way he carried himself, suggests he was a serious, almost frightening man. He was hardened by a life in the outdoors, making his way on mountain trails. He was a rugged, hairy, mountain man wearing a rough garment of black camel's hair fastened by a wide leather belt around his waist. Elijah was a wild man for God.

Elijah's name means, "My God is Yahweh." Yet, he was a common man who possessed an uncommon relationship with his God. The Bible declares, *"Elijah was a human being, even as we are. He prayed earnestly that it would not rain, and it did not rain on the land for three and a half years."*3 The great courage displayed by Elijah in his dealings with the evil Ahab and Jezebel was a direct result of his closeness with God through the Word and prayer. He knew God was with him and that he was sent by God as the tip of the spear to destroy the works of the devil. He was willing to risk his own life for this cause.

And so it was that this rugged man walked into the palace of King Ahab and Queen Jezebel and onto the pages of Bible history. He did not write fancy letters or send an advance team. He did not arrive in a limo, flanked by bodyguards and fawning supplicants. Elijah came out of the mountains alone and boldly stepped into the royal court. He looked this wicked monarch right in the eye and with the unction of God commanded an economy-killing drought that would last until he (Elijah) said otherwise. And it happened!

God Does Not Give Warning to Devils

When God decides to arise and scatter His enemies, He sends a "prophet," to confront evil and warn *people* of the consequences of their actions. God does not give warning to devils. He does not waste His time warning the kingdom of darkness and its powers, principalities and rulers of darkness. God destroys their works.

However, God gives warning and revelation to human beings out of pure love for us. God sends messages to men by using His message carriers – prophets. The Bible says, *"Surely the Lord God will do nothing, but he revealeth his secret unto his servants the prophets."*4 The prophets of God are spokesmen, messengers, watchmen and ambassadors who stand in the gap and build walls between God's people and evil. They are part of the five-fold ministry gifts to the Church: *"And he gave some apostles, and some prophets, and some evangelists, and some pastors, and teachers."*5

Prophets Flow in the Rhema Word

Prophets are gifted with the living (rhema) Word to the Church. We have learned that the Bible contains the *logos*, which is the written Word. But, when those words *come alive* in us, the logos is transformed into the rhema (life-giving word). This is the essence of spiritual revelation. It is a supernatural wellspring of information from God flowing into our being and when it happens, there is nothing Satan or his underlings can do to stop it.

Prophets *flow* in revelation or rhema. This process is a means for the Spirit of God to communicate with the Church. The Bible declares, *"He that hath an ear let him hear what the Spirit saith to the churches."*6 Therefore, the Lord desires to raise up prophets who will hear His voice and then, relay the message to the Church. *Prophets* means more than one. God wants many prophets in America.

Thus, the spiritual purpose of the *Elijah Awakening*.

God Wants Many Elijahs in America

God does not necessarily want "lone ranger" prophets. He will use only one if that is all He has, but He prefers to have a *prophetic people*. Moses declared, *"Would God that all the Lord's people were prophets and that the Lord would put his spirit upon them."*7 In this time of demonic oppression in America, it is imperative that many believers hear the Word of the Lord with the explosive power and energy that only comes from the prophetic anointing. There is tremendous power in numbers. The more, the merrier and the mightier!

The Elijah Awakening is a Revolution Against Evil

Prophets are God's spiritual reformers and revolutionaries. To reform means to bring about change. We need some big changes in America right now and the key to victory lies in the spiritual or supernatural realm. Prophets have been given vast spiritual authority to confront the kingdom of darkness and those who cooperate with it. God Himself said, *"… thou shalt go to all that I shall send thee, and whatsoever I command thee thou shalt speak. Be not afraid of their faces: for I am with thee to deliver thee, saith the Lord. … Behold, I have put my words in thy mouth. See, I have this day set thee over the nations and over the kingdoms, to root out, and to pull down, and to destroy, and to throw down, to build, and to plant."*8

In these verses, the word "nations" speaks to the *natural* realm. The word "kingdoms" speaks to the *supernatural* realm. To "root out" means to pull something out by its roots. Prophets are called to root out. They are called to pull down, destroy and overthrow. Notice that all these words deal with confronting and destroying things that are opposed to God and His Word.

Therefore, before any building and planting can take place, the evil has to be removed. God cannot bless a nation that is preoccupied with promoting the agenda of Jezebel and the evil of Baal. The wickedness must be destroyed before the good can flourish. Sin must be repented of before salvation can transform the lost. Bad ideas and evil laws and policies must be rooted out and pulled down.

When confronted, devils and evil men do not go quietly.

Jezebel Wanted to Murder Elijah

Prophets often cause violent reactions in those who embrace the doctrines of devils. This explains why evil-doers always try to get rid of or silence the prophet. This explains why Jezebel wanted to kill Elijah and murdered a great many of God's prophets. Throughout the Bible, the prophets of God were often opposed.

Jezebel sought to harm Elijah, but God did not allow it. Wild radicals in the streets of America will attempt to do us harm. The key is this: If we act on our own, evil can and will hurt us. But, if we are acting on the authority of God's orders and anointing, our steps are ordered by the Holy Spirit. Then, demons and violent radicals beware! God has plainly warned those who despise His prophets, *"Touch not mine anointed, and do my prophets no harm."⁹* Jesus said, *"Behold, I give unto you power to tread on serpents and scorpi-*

*ons, and over all the power of the enemy: and nothing shall by any means hurt you."*10

Supernatural Accounts Brought to Balance

As stated in the beginning of this book, the *Elijah Awakening* will bring a potent mixture of faithfulness to God and fearless prophetic activism that will challenge the agenda of Jezebel and Baalism in America. The real source of America's troubles emanate from malevolent enemies within the supernatural kingdom of Satan. War must be declared on these agents of darkness. Supernatural accounts must be brought to balance. This explains why God is about to regenerate the Church with an explosion of miracle power and authority to accomplish His purposes.

Signs and wonders will confirm the Word of the Lord as modern day American prophets will obey the directives of God to confront and destroy the works of a demonic system much like the prophet Elijah did so long ago. In Elijah's day, on orders from God, Jezebel was killed to crush her evil influence in the worship of Baal. Today, there is no Jezebel per se, but there is a Jezebel Agenda and Baalism exists. These things must be destroyed in America. Thus, the *Elijah Awakening* will advance the cause of Christ to the destruction of the kingdom of darkness from sea to shining sea.

Elijah's Miracles Revealed as Tactical Weapons

Finally, the following chapters of this book will unveil the miracles of Elijah as effective tactical weapons against Jezebel's agenda in ancient Israel and now, in America. Indeed, they have never lost their potency.

Miracle 1: *The Drought*
Miracle 2: *The Ravens*
Miracle 3: *A Woman and the Endless Supply*
Miracle 4: *Raising the Dead*
Miracle 5: *Calling Fire Down on the Altar*
Miracle 6: *Calling Down the Rain*
Miracle 7: *Calling Fire Down on Enemies*
Miracle 8: *Parting the Waters*
Miracle 9: *A Chariot of Fire and the Whirlwind*

9 Objectives for the Elijah Awakening in America

1. Prepare the way *as a forerunner* of the coming Lord. (Isaiah 40:3 KJV; Matthew 3:3 KJV).
2. Confront the Jezebel Agenda in both natural and supernatural realms. (Jeremiah 1:10 KJV).
3. Intercede in prayer for the nation. (Jeremiah 27:18 KJV).
4. Turn the hearts of fathers to their children. (Malachi 4:5-6 KJV).
5. Confront dead tradition and religions. (Matthew 3:9-10 KJV).
6. Reveal the mysteries of God to believers. (Ephesians 3:4-5 KJV).
7. Reveal or foretell future events. (Amos 3:7 KJV).
8. Intercede with fasting and prayer for God to remove territorial rulers of the dark kingdom over American cities and regions. (Daniel 10:1-21 KJV).
9. Prophesy to the nation. (Jeremiah 1:4-5 KJV).

CHAPTER THREE

The Drought

ELIJAH MIRACLE 1

"And Elijah the Tishbite, who was of the inhabitants of Gilead, said unto Ahab, 'As the Lord God of Israel liveth, before whom I stand, there shall not be dew nor rain these years, but according to my word." 1 Kings 17:1 KJV

The miracles performed by the prophet Elijah were as tactical weapons unleashed on Satan's dark kingdom. Through the agency of the prophet, the power of God exploded to humiliate and punish the enemy. In ancient Israel, God sought to rescue the people ensnared in a demonic religion, so He called Elijah out of a rugged mountain wilderness to declare war on the devil. His mission was to reveal the one true God to Israel and break the grip of evil in the nation. God wanted to get their attention, so Elijah called for a drought.

A Drought is a Prolonged Water Shortage

A drought is an event of prolonged water shortages. Severe droughts cause crop failures, famine, dust storms and malnutrition. It can quickly produce social unrest and mass migration out of affected areas. The historical record shows that Ancient Israel was a strongly agricultural society and relied on its farmers to produce food for the nation. They produced grains, grapes, dates, olives and more. They also kept herds of sheep and goats for milk and cheese. All of these agricultural pursuits require water and without it, none are possible. In other words, a drought would hit them where they lived.

At the outset of this Bible drama and without fanfare, Elijah walked into the courts of King Ahab and made three declarations: (1) the Lord God of Israel lives; (2) Elijah answers only to God; and (3) a drought would permeate the land until Elijah said otherwise. Elijah further characterized the drought at a level of severity such that, "...

there shall not be dew nor rain these years, but according to my word."1

A drought so severe that not a droplet of dew would moisten the soil was an economy killing, life-altering event to the nation of Israel. Thirty days without rain is not unusual in the Holy Land. Sixty days, while not deadly, is a serious issue. Ninety days is far worse. At the four month mark, serious signs of famine will appear. The drought of Elijah lasted three and a half *years*.

Israel was Devastated for Three and Half Years

During the third year of drought and famine, we can only imagine the suffering which was overwhelming the whole land. At this point, illness and death had decimated Israel. Milk and honey no longer flowed in the Promised Land. Starvation deepened and it affected men, women and children alike. The economy of Israel was obliterated.

Israel Tried to Worship both Baal and Jehovah

But God is the giver of both life and law. As such, He is a jealous God. "*Do not worship any other god, for the Lord, whose name is Jealous, is a jealous God.*"2 Israel had crossed the line when they turned to Baal, but still claimed a place with Jehovah. Superstitious fear, sexual rites and child sacrifice on the one hand against faith and loyalty on the other. Elijah angrily reprimanded them saying, *"..."How long will you waver between two opinions? If the LORD is God, follow him; but if Baal is God, follow him." But the people said nothing.*"3

The drought was a heavenly warning shot fired across Israel's bow.

Moses Gave the Law to Israel at Mt. Sinai

Sadly, Israel's history was filled with bad choices and disobedience to God. God brought them out of Egyptian bondage (the Exodus) and first gave them the law of Moses at Mt. Sinai. But, as a result of their idolatry, they were forced to wander in the wilderness until the Exodus generation died. Finally, they were brought to camp on the Jordan River in sight of Canaan – the Promised Land. After forty years of wandering in the wilderness, the new generation was ready to enter Canaan. Moses brought them together for one last admonition, recorded in the Book of Deuteronomy.

Moses Gave the Law a Second Time and a Dire Warning

The name *Deuteronomy* means, "second law." Here, Moses gave the Law a second time. He reminded them of Israel's past rebellion and the grace of God up to that point. He urged them to remain faithful to God. In great detail, Moses explained the Law for Israel's spiritual worship, leadership and social life. At the end of this final discourse, Moses gave them a dire warning: *"Be careful, or you will be enticed to turn away and worship other gods and bow down to them. Then the LORD's anger will burn against you, and he will shut up the heavens so that it will not rain and the ground will yield no produce, and you will soon perish from the good land the LORD is giving you."*4

Israel had been put on notice. They should have known better. The drought was forewarned by Moses as a severe punishment for worshiping strange gods. It was the only miracle of Elijah that held this punitive distinction.

No Man can Serve Two Masters

Yet some five hundred years later, Israel allowed the power hungry Jezebel, along with the feckless King Ahab to entice them into disobedience and idolatry. As promised, God's anger burned against them and the heavens were shut so that no rain fell upon the land. Israel provoked God by trying to have their cake and eat it too. They wanted blessings from the throne of God *and* from the throne of the dark ruler of Baalism.

But no man can serve two masters.

Neither Joe Biden or King Ahab were God's Best Choices

Joe Biden, dubious winner of the 2020 presidential election and arguably, a guy who never met a communist he didn't like, stumbled across the trip wires of Almighty God when he touched the Holy Bible on January of 2021. Alas, Biden was never God's best choice for America, just as Ahab was never God's best choice for Israel.

The fearsome cherubim guarding the throne of God went on full alert when Biden *touched* the throne of God by placing his hand on the Holy Bible to swear an oath. Some believe Biden did not use a genuine Bible, but a Satanic book with upside down crosses on it. However, it was reported that he used an old family Bible with Celtic crosses on it. It is the opinion of this writer that a family Bible was used. Therefore, the public display of placing a hand on it, while swearing an oath, may have been tantamount to a wrongful touching of the *Ark of God.* It follows that such an act was akin to flipping a "supernatural switch" that would provoke a jealous and righteous God.

To understand this, we must observe the Ark of the Covenant.

The Old Testament Ark of God (or the Ark of the Covenant) was a gold-covered, wooden chest that contained the Ten Commandments on stone tablets given to Moses.5 It also contained Aaron's rod and a golden jar of manna.5 When the Israelites marched for the Promised Land, the Ark was carried in the lead preceding the people and was the signal for their advance.

The Ark of God was a Holy Thing

The power and glory of God emanated from the Ark. Two golden cherubs guarded the space known as the "mercy seat" on its lid. Because the Lord's presence was in this space, God was *enthroned* between the cherubim.6 Thus, the Ark was a holy thing.

When they crossed a river, the river dried up as soon as the feet of the priests carrying the Ark touched its waters, and it remained dry until the Ark left the river after the people passed over.7 Indeed, the Ark brought Divine blessing, but if it was handled improperly, God's judgment and curses exploded on the perpetrators.

A Death Warning for Touching the Ark

The Ark was carried by way of staves made of shittim wood that would be placed through rings that were attached to its four corners. God commanded that the staves not be removed from the rings.8 A death warning was issued to the bearers of the Ark not to touch it, a *"... holy thing, lest they die."*9

But the Ark *was touched* and the man's life was taken by God because of it. As the Ark was being transported, the oxen pulling the cart stumbled and a man called Uzzah *took hold of the Ark.* The Scriptures record that God's anger burned against Uzzah and he died instantly.10

Further mistreatment of the Ark brought swift reaction by God. According to the Scriptural record, the Ark was captured in a battle against the heathen Philistines and placed in a temple of the Canaanite god Dagon. The next morning, the false god was found on the floor, bowed down before the Ark. Upon restoring Dagon to an upright position, he was on the next morning again found prostrate and broken. The heathen people were smitten with tumors and a plague of mice.11 Then, an affliction of boils came upon them.12 After seven months, the Philistines, thoroughly chastised by God, gladly returned the Ark to the Israelites.13 There is a strong spiritual lesson in this for those who would steal presidential elections.

The Bible Represents the Throne of God

The Bible is the spiritual Ark of the Covenant today. It is the infallible Word of God. Because God is *enthroned* in His Word, the Bible represents the throne of God.

What are the supernatural risks when one "touches" the throne of God with one hand and caresses the demonic throne of Baalism with the other? During his small inauguration, Joe Biden reached out and placed his hand on the *spiritual throne* of God to swear the oath of office. Biden did this while also pledging to use his vast authority for evil works that defy Almighty God and blaspheme His name.

These evil works include:

- Slaughtering babies in the womb.
- Destroying masculinity, femininity, marriage.
- Putting LGBTQ+ people in leadership.
- Justifying transgender activity and allow males who identify as women to compete in women's sports.
- Giving US. international-aid money to overseas groups that promote or perform abortions.

The Joe Biden Debacle Opened a Pandora's Box

By allowing the highly suspect debacle of the 2020 Joe Biden presidential election to take root, America's elected leaders stupidly opened a demonic Pandora's Box. What fresh hell now flows from the open sewers that seem to comprise the executive, legislative and judicial branches of our government? Evil leftists should gird their loins, because God is not having any of it. *"But if any nation does not listen, I will completely uproot and destroy it,"* declares the Lord.*"*14 Indeed, God does not suffer idolatry and He has not changed His mind about it. He is the same yesterday, today and forever. We ignore this at our peril.

Evildoers in America need to brace for what is coming next.

Idolatry as an Economic Issue

Idolatry can manifest as an economic issue (think: Biden's socialist economy agenda). The great attraction to Baal wasn't just wild sex orgies under every green tree; it was also an economic attraction. Baal, the fertility and nature god, was known as the "rider of the clouds," who made the rains to fall and the land to prosper. Israel was beguiled into believing, right along with the Canaanites, that Baal was the true source of "milk and honey" in the Promised Land. This was a tragic mistake.

God's "boycott" on Israel's prosperity

As a result, God launched a "boycott" on the prosperity of the nation by withholding the blessing of rain. The land depends on rain to sustain it: *"But the land you are crossing the Jordan to take possession of is a land of mountains and valleys that drinks rain from heaven."*15 There are no large rivers in Canaan to use for irrigation. So, Israel depended on rain as their main source of water. In this, rain is a type of blessing that will promote the harvest.

Therefore, rain can establish prosperity. But, Israel ignored Jehovah and gave credit to the demon god Baal for the rain. God reacted swiftly to this blasphemy. The resulting drought crushed them like a bug. It affected every human and every business. It affected King Ahab and Queen Jezebel. And, it discredited Baal, the "rider of the clouds."

In Sleepy Joe's radicalized America, Baal needs to be discredited again.

Supernatural Agency: Calling the End Result into Existence

The *Elijah Awakening* in America will stir in believers the unshakable realization of their potential to work the works of Christ. Jesus declared, *"Very truly I tell you, whoever believes in me will do the works I have been doing, and they will do even greater things than these, because I am going to the Father."*16 Christ has bequeathed to us the supernatural ability to do even greater works than He did as proof that Jesus is the union between God in heaven and the believer on earth. When He was hanged on Calvary's cross, his arms outstretched, Jesus took the sinful hand of man and the perfect holy hand of God and put them together on his bloody chest, and sobbed, *"It is finished."*17 There, on Golgotha's hill, the anointing of the Christ broke the yoke of Satan and a supernatural path to the blessing and power of God was established for humanity once again.

Now watch this.

Through the Bible, God never does anything in the earth until He first speaks it. It must be spoken, prophesied or called for in the prayer of faith. He, *"... calleth those things which be not as though they were."*18 In the Lord's Prayer, Christ taught us to pray, *"...Thy will be done in earth, as it is in heaven..."*19 Jesus saw what His Father was doing in heaven and then did it on earth.20 Once the will of God is revealed to us (i.e., prophecy or prayer), we can pray it will happen on earth. We can call the end result into existence. We can know the will of God because we have the mind of Christ. We can think like Jesus. Paul said, *"... we have the mind of Christ."*21

But, there is one more action step.

The Law of Binding and Loosing

The people of God must learn to utilize the law of binding and loosing. Jesus declared, *"I will give you the keys of the kingdom of heaven; whatever you bind on earth will be bound in heaven, and whatever you loose on earth will be loosed in heaven."* 22 The keys for binding and loosing are not for initiating action, but rather are for *enacting things already ordained in heaven.*

These keys give believers the authority on earth to perform the will of God (in heaven). They are the means by which we will call those things which be not as though they are. We will use them to unleash on the earth powerful weapons that have already been ordained in heaven for our use in the fight against the kingdom of darkness. By faith, we will reach into the invisible kingdom of God, take hold of whatever we need and pull it through the veil into the physical realm.

In the coming revival, the Holy Spirit will awaken mighty warriors to pray and believe that God will do the impossible in their nation. To test the unfathomable resources of God, we must leap by faith into the impossible. The *Elijah Awakening* will ignite spiritual warriors who will call into existence the drought and famine of God to wreak havoc on the financial strongholds of the kingdom of darkness. We will bind the power of the dark rulers of Baalism by loosing the power of Almighty God in our land. Let the wealth of the wicked be turned to the righteous and to God be the glory.

Human Agency: Calling the Drought on Leftist Businesses

In the meantime, believers should rise up as agents of God and wade into the earthly dynamics of *fighting the good fight*. A "drought" or boycott should be brought to bear on every business that supports the "woke cancel culture." Patriots should withhold the "rain" of financial blessing from them all. Let them dry up and blow away in the winds of God.

Patriots must institute a "drought" against every politician who refuses to stand for the laws of God. If they bow to Baal by supporting sexual freedom, gender identity rights, abortion rights and so on, put them on the "drought list." If they want to strip Americans of their constitutional rights (1st and 2nd Amendments, states rights, etc.) with legislation, they should be legally removed from office. This would likely include each and every Democrat in the US House of Representatives and the US Senate. Globalist RINO Republicans who vote with Democrats on issues that defy the Word of God belong on the drought list too. An election "famine" must drive these evil politicians out of office.

Calling the Drought on Fake News Media and Big Tech Social Media

Big television media companies live and die by audience ratings and advertisers. Patriots must stop watching fake news shows thus allowing their ratings numbers to fall into the abyss. Cast them and their demonic leftist propaganda into outer darkness. We must cease buying products from each and every one of their leftist advertisers.

The Scripture declares, *"...the wealth of the wicked is stored up for the righteous."*23 Without doing violence to the Scriptures, let it be also said that the wicked get wealth when we take it from our storehouses and give it to them. It is time for the drought of God to dry them up. Leave that hard-earned money in your pocket. Shake these evil companies off like the dust from your feet!

Next, there is simply no place for leftist social media to obstruct our freedom of speech. They should go the way of the Dodo bird. They need to become financially extinct. Period. There are plenty of great up and coming platforms for social media that support the freedom of speech and open discourse for patriots. Places where Christian conservatives are welcome and where patriots who love America *as founded* are welcome. Use them instead of evil platforms created by the prophets of Baal in the social media world. Let the drought of God bring a great famine to the kingdom of darkness in America.

CHAPTER FOUR

The Ravens

ELIJAH MIRACLE 2

"And the ravens brought him bread and flesh in the morning, and bread and flesh in the evening; and he drank from the brook." 1 Kings 17:6 KJV

We are about to witness an explosive spiritual awakening in a magnificent testimony to the One who was raised from the dead on the third day. The Gospel of Jesus Christ will come alive to millions of Americans in a time of finishing grace, when the Spirit of God will be poured out upon all flesh. But, in this atmosphere of spiritual renewal, the *Elijah Awakening* will mobilize the

71

soldiers of Christ in an epic spiritual confrontation with evil in America from sea to shining sea.

Genuine Revival May be Gauged by Its Opposition

Interestingly, the success of a genuine spiritual revival may be gauged by the degree of opposition arrayed against it. Such opposition will present itself in the form of devils and men. The more powerful the revival grows, the more opposition will line up against it. But *"where the Spirit of the Lord is, there is liberty."*1 In this, we can know that whatever opposes us can also define us; a concept the American Church has often failed to grasp over the years in its childlike search for gain without pain. Indeed, war makes fighting men and women out of boys and girls. The coming conflict will change us forever because freedom is not free. It will cost us something.

Consider the cost to Elijah when he challenged the kingdom of darkness.

God puts Elijah into Witness Protection

The prophet of God boldly walked into the court of King Ahab and Queen Jezebel, and without fanfare, informed them that the dew and rain would cease falling for *years,* subject to his word alone. The prophet then quickly departed. No doubt Jezebel flew into a spluttering rage and wanted him executed immediately for such impertinence. But the purposes of God were not deterred by the tantrums of a screaming psychotic. The Lord simply whisked Elijah away into a Divine witness protection program.

Elijah was instructed by God: "*Get away from here and turn eastward, and hide by the brook Cherith, which flows into the Jordan. And it will be that you shall drink from the brook, and I have commanded the ravens to feed you there.*"2 So, Elijah *went and did* according to the word of the Lord and there, he was fed by ravens.

Raven are Scavengers but God Uses Them

Ravens are black birds closely related to crows, except much larger. In fact, they are the largest perching bird in the world with wingspans up to 50 inches. Ravens are found worldwide from the arctic to the deserts of North Africa to the Pacific islands. They are among the most intelligent of birds. They are capable of aerial acrobatics and can mimic human speech. They eat berries, fruit, insects, bread and carrion. They kill and eat small birds and mammals such as rabbits and rats. Most notably, ravens are scavengers.

Yet, God uses ravens.

The Bible tells us that when the floodwaters began to recede, Noah released a raven to search for dry land.3 Flying over a flood was no problem for the raven who survived by scavenging food floating on the surface of the waters. The Bible says God cares for the ravens and *"... provides food for... the young ravens when they call."*4 Jesus mentioned them saying, *"Consider the ravens: They do not sow or reap, they have no storeroom or barn; yet God feeds them..."*5 So God fed the ravens and the ravens fed Elijah.

God's Ravens are Detestable

When God gave the Law to Moses, He declared that ravens were not to be eaten because they were unclean birds: *"And these you shall detest among the birds; they shall not be eaten; they are detestable..."*6 Ravens were detestable and not to be consumed under any circumstances. This fact makes God's choice of ravens to feed Elijah very intriguing.

How thrilled Elijah must have been to realize that he was now a wanted fugitive on the run, camped out by a small brook in a ravine to the east of the Jordan river. It was bad enough to be forced to hide in dusty desolation, but to be dependent on scavenger birds to bring him breakfast and supper was beyond comprehension! Moreover, it is not normal for wild ravens to come near a human with bread and meat in their beaks. But God commanded these *detestable* birds to do just that.

Destable has a Similar Vibe to "Deplorable"

The term "detestable" has a vibe that is similar to the word *deplorable*. In 2016, it was widely reported that at a fundraising event, Hillary Clinton infamously slandered Americans who supported Donald J. Trump by claiming they belonged in a "basket of deplorables." The Trump campaign wisely began to repeatedly use the phrase against Clinton during and after the 2016 presidential election. Later, the phrase was shortened to the single term "deplorables."

Other slur-bombs against the "deplorables" had been thrown years earlier. In 2008, it was widely reported that Barack Obama vomited his hatred by slamming conservatives as "bitter clingers," who loved Bibles and guns. Sleepy Joe used the term "Neanderthal thinking" to criticize the Texas governor's move to end Covid mask mandates. Since the Capitol protests on January 6, 2021, fake news media and minions of some of the vaunted alphabet agencies have accused President Trump and his supporters as "domestic terrorists."

By this wild logic, the prophet Elijah would have been labeled a domestic terrorist and his name put on the Left's list of enemies. The miracles he performed by the power of Almighty God would have been labeled as "acts of terror" or "insurrection" by today's elitist justice standards. The alphabet agencies would have wanted to haul him in for interrogation and imprisonment. Indeed, this demonic vitriol by the Left is far more sinister than simply name calling.

Radical leftists want to destroy any person who does not toe their line. They and their fake news media apologists soft-pedal their evil actions as "progressive policies," but, in reality, they are simply part of the same China, Cuba and Russia communist playbooks. Arrests and re-education camps for Trump supporters may not be that far-fetched if these lunatics can bring their Jezebel Agenda into the fullness of its hellish potential. The inescapable truth is that elitist Democrats, leftist lunatics and RINOs appear to stand together as a "Uniparty" in their demonic hatred of the MAGA deplorables in Joe Biden's "woke" America.

However, God's warriors refused to bow to Baal. To the abject horror of the Left, Donald Trump's America First, MAGA supporters happily adopted the moniker "deplorables" to describe themselves. Tee-shirts, baseball caps and bumper stickers were printed and sold by the truckloads.

In fact, to be called a "deplorable" is now a badge of honor to God-fearing, country loving, conservatives in America.

What does this have to do with Elijah?

God Will Use the Deplorables to "Bring the Receipts"

Just as God used "detestables" to bring meat and bread to Elijah during the initial stages of his battle with Jezebel, God will use "deplorables" to aid the *Elijah Awakening* in confronting evil. As spiritual warfare explodes across the hellish landscape of Sleepy Joe's dictatorship, God will again send the ravens – decent Americans slandered by Washington elites as unwashed, unenlightened, unimportant *deplorables,* to "bring the receipts" to the front lines of a fiery supernatural battle.

A Warrior Giant of Patriotic Believers Will Arise

So far, we have witnessed only the beginning skirmishes in a war against the kingdom of darkness that will escalate into a supernatural conflict of Biblical proportions nationwide. When the coming spiritual renewal is ignited by a heavenly explosion of Holy Ghost power, a warrior giant of millions of patriotic American believers will awaken and enter the fray. When God's warriors take the field of battle, they will need adequate provisions. They will need God's ravens to see them through.

So it was that Elijah needed sustenance. Thus, God sent the ravens to feed him twice a day. The prophet received meat and bread in the morning and again, in the evening. The ravens did not bring enough to last for a week. They brought just enough to keep Elijah going for one day at a time and no more.

God is a One Day at a Time God

According to dietary studies, a relatively sedentary man aged anywhere from 26 to 40 years old requires 2,400 calories per day to stay alive. Other studies have shown that a person eating fewer than 1000 calories per day is, for all practical purposes, starving. But the heart of God is good and Elijah did not starve. He cared for His prophet each day. Jesus prayed, *"Give us today our daily bread."*7 God is a one day at a time God. Whatever the ravens brought, it was good for Elijah to eat and in just the right amount, at just the right time.

God Sent Elijah a Heavenly Dietitian

Later in Elijah's adventure, God sent an angel as a sort of heavenly dietitian to make sure Elijah ate enough.8 The angel instructed the prophet to eat more to prepare him for the hard journey ahead. Therefore, if God can send ravens and angels to provide and supervise daily food requirements for Elijah, he will surely take care of us in the coming days.

Before Elijah Could Stand, He Had To Sit

So, God taught Elijah to trust him on a daily basis until he could live in a place of total reliance on God. Americans pride themselves on self-reliance, but in a supernatural fight with the kingdom of darkness we must learn to rely on God more than we rely on our own abilities. When most people think of Elijah, they think of him challenging the evil prophets of Baal at Mount Carmel and calling down the fire. But before Elijah could stand on Mount Carmel, he needed to sit by the brook Cherith. American believers would do well to spend some time sitting by the brook.

For it was at the brook, that things took an interesting turn.

Elijah Drank from the Brook and the Brook Dried Up

God told Elijah, *"And it shall be, that thou shalt drink of the brook…"*9 Please take note that God did not chose to supply Elijah's needs with a river, or a lake, or an artesian well. Instead, Elijah was instructed to lap water from a small brook in the midst of a drought. This was a temporary solution at best because the dwindling brook would soon dry up and Elijah, the hardy mountain man, knew it. But he trusted God and stayed by the brook and drank its water when he was thirsty.

But then, it all changed. The Bible states, *"And it came to pass after a while, that the brook dried up, because there had been no rain in the land."*10 The words "dried up" indicate a progressive reduction of water flow. Elijah did not wake up one morning to find the stream gone. It took some time for this flow to cease.

It is unknown how long Elijah was camped by the brook Cherith. It could have been several months. Meanwhile, the drought burned up the earth. Day after day, while eagerly searching the skies for ravens, Elijah watched the dwindling water flow, endured the heat and considered the terrible drought. Maybe he blamed himself for the hardships he now faced. After all, Elijah was the reason the rain stopped in the first place.

Elijah was Caught in the Whirlwind of His Own Destiny

He was a man caught in the whirlwind of his own destiny. Elijah did not ask for this dangerous assignment. Instead, he was snatched by God out of his quiet existence in the mountains and sent to prophesy an unpopular message to an evil, feckless king and his murderous wife. To his credit, Elijah wanted to prove that Baal, "the rider of the clouds," was powerless against the will of Jehovah. But he was human and may have had second thoughts about the great risks involved.

Even Jesus had second thoughts in His final days on earth. He knew the will of God would crush Him at Calvary's cross and, in His humanity, prayed for the Father to *"...take this cup from me..."*11 Yet, Christ fulfilled His purpose and died on that cross to save mankind. Elijah would have much rather stayed in his mountain home, but he knew what God wanted him to do and that was to motivate Israel to turn back to the Lord. So, Elijah obeyed God and prayed for the rain to stop. But, when the rain stopped, the land burned up, people suffered terribly and Elijah suffered right along with them.

Sometimes, God has to bring *all* of us to our knees to get *some* of us back on our feet.

Something Supernatural This Way Comes

America will never be great again until the Church comes awake again. America was founded on the principles of God. But for decades, the Church cowered on the sidelines and watched while devils ran wild and laid waste to our beliefs and changed our laws, shaking their fists in God's face. In the spirit of Jezebel, America enthusiastically worshiped sex, drugs and music – the building blocks of Baalism – but not God. This is sad, but true.

However, as Bob Dylan might sing, "The times they are a-changin." God is not finished with America just yet. The heavenly winds of revival are starting to blow in our direction. Something huge is coming and the Church needs to get ready for it.

Revival Will Help Americans Believe Their Beliefs Again

Revival is a supernatural event, which manifests in an eye-opening recognition of and reconciliation with Almighty God. Real revival shakes people right down to their core. It makes whole-hearted believers out of them. Real revival will help Americans to start believing their beliefs again.

Christians used to sing about being lifted up, above the shadows. A genuine spiritual revival will lift the Church up above the stench of the Biden presidency, the curse of Baalism and the kingdom of darkness in America. When the Church is revived, believers will be lifted into the unfathomable love of God and His power from on high. Indeed, something supernatural is about to happen that will offset the tragedy and loss and pain we have gone through. We need to get ready to hear what the Spirit is about to say to the churches in America.

The Supernatural Door Opens

Sometimes, the only way God can get our attention is to allow our brook to run dry. It is the only way to get us off our spiritual backsides and make us pray our way into the next level of blessing. Then, we will be ready to receive the water turned into wine He has for us. Then, our next moves can be mapped out by the Master and we can flow into our destinies. Then, the strongholds of Baalism can be pulled down in America.

When Elijah's brook dried up, a supernatural door was opened to him. The water stopped and in the next instant, the Bible says, *"Then the word of the LORD came to him: Go at once to Zarephath in the region of Sidon and stay there. I have directed a widow there to supply you with food."* 12 America, now more than ever, needs God to open a door for us. Like Elijah, we need to leave the dried up creek bottom in our lives and go at once to Zarapheth.

The Last Place the Devil Would Ever Think to Look

Zarephath, known as Sarepta in Luke's gospel, was thought by the Jewish historian Josephus, to have been located on the coast road between Tyre and Sidon. This region was within the dominion of Ethbaal, the father of Jezebel. It was a stronghold of Baalism and an unfriendly territory. Yet God chose this place to send His prophet. In doing so, God sent Elijah straight into the heart of darkness. But such are the purposes of God, for the will of God cuts through the rocks and thorny places. God makes a way where there seems to be no way. Thus, at a time when the land of Israel was apostate and unsafe, God found a safe harbor for His prophet in the home country of his deadliest enemy, Jezebel.

God sent Elijah to the last place the devil would ever think to look.

CHAPTER FIVE

A Woman and the Endless Supply

ELIJAH MIRACLE 3

"For thus saith the Lord, the God of Israel,
'The barrel of meal shall not waste, neither
shall the cruse of oil fail, until the day that
the LORD sendeth rain upon the earth.'" 1
Kings 17:14 KJV

A supernatural hunt for a certain type of spiritual warrior is underway in our nation. Almighty God is searching for women who will believe Him more than they believe the lunatics and liars on fake news shows. God needs mothers and grandmothers and daughters and sisters of the heavenly kingdom who know how to pray and make war on hell. He seeks fearless female warriors that are unafraid of a "woke" cancel culture, thugs posing as pro-testers, negative peer pressure and persecution. The Lord wants women who fit a certain spiritual profile who can put on the whole armor of God. He seeks women who understand the deep things of God and will do His will. Like the widow in Zarephath, God searches for faithful women He can count on in the coming days of the *Elijah Awakening*.

Jesus held Women in High Regard

God places high value on the contributions of women. This was evidenced by the actions of Jesus during His earthly ministry. The Master often encountered women along the way to Calvary's cross. An example of Jesus' high regard for them occurred in Bethany a few days before the final Passover of His life. Jesus and the disciples were rest-ing in the house of a friend. As He reclined at a table, a woman (Mary, the sister of Lazarus) approached Him with an alabaster jar of expensive perfume called Spikenard and poured some of it on Him. The disciples were agitated by this apparent waste and sought to admonish the woman for not selling the perfume and giving the money as an offer-ing, but Christ stopped them saying, *"By pouring this per-fume on Me, she has prepared My body for burial. Truly I tell* *you, wherever this gospel is preached in all the world, what she has done will also be told in memory of her."*1 In this, we can understand that God places a high premium on humility and love. These characteristics are precisely the reason that the starving, yet selfless widow who humbly ministered to the prophet Elijah is also well remembered after thousands of years.

The story of the widow of Zarephath is one of sacrificial devotion to the needs of others. It is a story of obedience to the God of Israel; a God she did not know. Finally, it is about the miracle God worked for her that would change her life forever.

Because Israel bowed to pagan idols, God sent Elijah to Samaria, into the court of King Ahab and Jezebel to initiate a supernatural confrontation with evil by stopping the rain for three and half years. A hideous drought ensued and dark desolation permeated the land. This only worsened when Jezebel began to ramp up the demonic worship of Baal. She also began killing the prophets of Jehovah. As a result, Elijah was forced to run for his life.

God sent Elijah to the Widow in Jezebel's Home Territory

The Lord sent him first to the brook Cherith where the ravens fed him for weeks and maybe months. Then, when the brook dried up, God gave Elijah new instructions saying, *"Go at once to Zarephath in the region of Sidon and stay there. I have directed a widow there to supply you with food."* 2 In the previous chapter, we learned that God sent the prophet right into Jezebel's territory. This was a dangerous proposition, but Elijah needed assistance and God had already prepared just the right person to do the job – the widow of Zarephath. Certainly, Elijah needed her help, but even more importantly, she needed Elijah.

Bible facts about the widow of Zarephath:

- She was a widow with a young son. Her husband may have died from starvation during the famine.
- She was from a city in Sidon (Lebanon today) within the kingdom of Ethbaal, father of Jezebel.
- She was not an Israelite subject to the Law of Moses.
- She lived in a house with an upper loft area that was used to house Elijah.

- God knew her heart and the desperate situation she faced and prepared her to be used as His instrument.
- She and her son were dying of starvation and had nearly run out of food when Elijah found her.
- Elijah lived in her household during the drought and famine.
- Her son would soon die and be raised from the dead by Elijah (see next chapter).

The Widow was Gathering Sticks at the City Gate

So, in spite of the fact that Zarephath was deep in the heart of Jezebel's home turf, the Bible records that Elijah arose and went there. When he came to the gate of the city, the prophet saw this woman gathering sticks to make a fire. It is likely she was too weak from hunger to gather wood farther away than the gate area. In the scorching heat, this lady was dehydrated and suffering. It was here at the gate that Elijah did something that at first, seemed insensitive. *"He called to her and asked, 'Would you bring me a little water in a jar so I may have a drink?'"*3 The Scriptures record that she dutifully went to get it, but again Elijah called to her, *"And bring me, please, a piece of bread."*3 This poor widow was struggling physically and mentally, yet

Elijah ignored these factors to ask her to fetch him bread and water. She was essentially out of food and the energy it took to fetch it. Her entire life was burning up in the horrendous drought and resulting famine. Why would Elijah make such a request of one so reduced by hardship?

The answer is spiritually profound: God used Elijah to help propel this woman into her miraculous destiny.

The Widow's Elijah Awakening

It is also important to understand that this woman did not know Elijah, but she *expected* him by the revelation of God. The NIV Bible indicates that God had *"directed"* her to supply the prophet. The King James version states that God *"commanded"* her to provide for Elijah. Either way, the will of God permeated her spirit, enabling her so that she actualized a Divine purpose to help Elijah even at the risk of sacrificing herself and her son. Thus enlightened, this good woman realized that God wanted her to give all she had and trust Him for the rest. This was the moment of her *Elijah Awakening* when God called her into action.

Her heart was open to the plan of God. She wanted to obey. Something deep inside of her was propelling her into a blessing she could not yet fathom. She was almost ready to lay it all on the line, but first needed to make sure Elijah was aware of her situation – a last minute hesitation before taking a leap of faith. So, she told the prophet that she did not have a loaf of bread, but only a handful of flour in a jar and a little oil in a jug. She laid her worst fears at his feet by saying, *"I am gathering a few sticks to take home and make a meal for myself and my son, that we may eat it—and die."*4

Jobless Americans are Gathering Sticks at the City Gate

In America, thousands of jobless Americans have been reduced to gathering sticks at the gate of the city. During the over-hyped Coronavirus pandemic of 2020, the American economy was crushed by the madness of nation-wide lockdowns. Then, using the pandemic as cover, radical Democrats and their co-conspirators allegedly pulled off the greatest election heist in American history. While millions of Americans cried foul, many of our elected representatives simply stood by and watched the show. Even the Vice-President and the US Supreme Court played possum while the Republic was eviscerated. In God's time, the truth will be revealed.

On his first doubtful day in office as president, Joe Biden destroyed tens of thousands of American jobs (added to the millions already out of work due to the Covid 19 pandemic) with the stroke of his pen by canceling the Keystone Pipeline and banning new fracking on federal land. Then, Biden signed another executive order to rejoin the Paris Climate Accord. In effect, such leftist lunacy will cost even more American jobs as the "Party of Davos" globalist elites would now be allowed to dictate what American companies do. American corporations will likely begin to move American jobs overseas.

Every Town is a Border Town

With the end of this madness nowhere in sight, the Biden regime has continued its wretched policy of allowing hundreds of thousands of desperate illegals into the promised land of America. Mexican drug and human trafficking cartels rejoiced at their prospects for financial windfalls from this illicit and dangerous policy. It was also alleged that the Biden regime has secretly (and illegally) used the US military to transport and resettle illegals in America's heartland, primarily in red states. Americans from every corner of the country have cried foul. Every town in America is a border town. It appears that the Biden regime is desperate to fundamentally change America against the will of the American people.

It was widely reported in early 2021, that Biden designated his cackling VP Kamala Harris to oversee efforts to stem the flow of illegal aliens at the southern border. Harris' aides immediately sought to temper this announcement by claiming Harris was "not doing the border," rather her focus would be on "root causes of migration." What could that possibly mean? After some 100 days of inaction, Harris finally visited El Paso, Texas, but has gone nowhere near the worst "hot spots" on the Texas southern border hundreds of miles away. In fact, her useless visit was only announced after it was reported that Donald Trump would visit the Texas/Mexico border himself in late June, 2021. Interestingly, some congressional Republicans, like disgruntled school children, have postured, signed petitions and held meaningless press conferences with great gusto, calling for Harris' removal as the border czar.

Meanwhile, Biden and his radical handlers may want to provide voting rights and societal benefits for all. Of course, this is likely a shifty shell game to garner the votes of beholden illegals to help radical Democrats win future elections. Soon, the middle class will be erased by the financial drought caused by these anti-America policies. Thus, America will become Venezuela. There will only be two classes: rich and poor. The rich will get richer and the poor will fight over sticks at the gate of the city.

The Widow Gently Pushed into Her Destiny

And so it was, that the widow of Zarephath was hideously reduced by the great drought to gathering sticks for her last meal. She was weakened and distressed. But there was something inside of her frail humanity that saw a glimmer of hope for a blessing somewhere in her future. She needed a gentle push into her destiny.

And Elijah was sent by God, at that time, in that place, to give it to her.

This explains why the great prophet pressed her further, *"… Don't be afraid. Go home and do as you have said. But first make a small loaf of bread for me from what you have and bring it to me, and then make something for yourself and your son."*5 The miracle process of God is found herein: *"Give and it shall be given to you…"*6 But there is something more: *"Honour the LORD with thy substance, and with the firstfruits of all thine increase."*7 Notice the order. First, take care of God's business, then your business. This explains why Elijah requested that she FIRST make bread for him, then for herself. But this woman was on her last legs. How could she give "firstfruits" from an "increase" she did not possess? In fact, she was gathering sticks for her last meal! As a human being, her first instinct on the human wavelength would be to care for her son. But she was operating on a supernatural wavelength. Her first instinct, in the Spirit, was to care for the things of God. Jesus said, *"But seek first his kingdom and his righteousness, and all these things will be given to you as well."*8 When God's cause is made the first objective, then all the rest in our lives will fall into place.

The Secret to the Endless Supply of God

Then comes back the Word of God: *"Now faith is the substance of things hoped for, the evidence of things not seen."*9 By faith, the widow gave Elijah the first portion of an increase she did not yet have – a miracle supply of food hoped for and not yet seen!

So, it is here we discover the hidden secret to the endless supply: *God will provide to us the faith we do not have.*

The Lord requires faith to move the mountain when He knows we do not have it. But, He loves us so much that by His Spirit, He gives us all the faith we need and the mountain moves. It is *"...not by might, nor by power, but by my Spirit, says the Lord Almighty."*10 God does all the heavy lifting. What a wonderful Lord we have!

Now watch what happens next.

As the widow turned to fetch the food in the faith God gave her, the host of heaven watched with great interest as Elijah spoke the prophetic word of the Lord to her: *"For* *this is what the LORD, the God of Israel, says: 'The jar of flour will not be used up and the jug of oil will not run dry until the day the LORD sends rain on the land.'"*11 Boom! The miracle exploded into reality. The Lord granted this humble and obedient woman an endless supply until the famine ended.

A Great Shaking is Coming to America

Soon, a great shaking will occur, evidenced by darkening financial conditions. The US government will run the presses to print money on worthless paper with no means to pay for any of it. Inflation will rise just like the hot air coming out of the White House. Mortgages rates will rise. Costs will rise. This will result in a demand for higher worker incomes that will cause greedy globalist corporations to respond by shipping American jobs overseas, putting more Americans out of work. The famine is coming and many will not be prepared for what it will bring.

God Establishes the Foundations of His purpose in America

As God once shook ancient Israel in the days of Elijah, so shall America be shaken in the coming days. When God decides to send His delivering power, He shakes the foundations of Satan's kingdom. In doing so, God establishes the mighty foundations of His purpose. He knows we can never achieve His perfect plan until every vain imagination has been removed.

God will provide for those who believe Him more than they believe anything else. He is seeking those who will give their all for Him. When the widow of Zarephath gave Elijah the last food she had, God provided a supply of food that lasted until the rains came again. In the *Elijah Awakening*, all things will be possible to those who believe God in the dark days ahead, even during the worst famine.

Women are Flashpoints in the Elijah Awakening

Finally, women will be flashpoints for the *Elijah Awakening*. God uses human agency to accomplish His purposes in the earth and women warriors of the faith will figure greatly in the coming days. It matters not if God asks some to be in supportive roles or lead armies into battle, men and women stand as equals before God. Both are made in the image of God. Neither is inferior to the other. In the coming days, Godly women will work miracles to fulfill their supernatural destinies in the battle for the soul of America.

They will run and not be weary. They will walk and not faint. When the women of God move into alignment with His purposes, God may even raise the dead to make a way where there seemed to be no way.

And that is exactly what happened next in Zarephath.

CHAPTER SIX

Raising the Dead

ELIJAH MIRACLE 4

*"And the Lord heard the voice of Elijah; and
the soul of the child came into him again,
and he revived."* 1 Kings 17:22 KJV

Sometimes, God needs to turn our world upside down
to position us for miracles. We can celebrate great
victories, yet suddenly find ourselves surrounded by
the devil's imps aiming to do serious harm. Similarly, in
the midst of the famine of ancient Israel, the widow of
Zarephath and her son had just been saved from starvation
by a supernatural miracle. Their food supplies were contin-
ually replenished and their lives continued. Then suddenly,

the widow's son became ill and died even though Elijah was living in the same house!

This story proves that anything can happen on this marvelous journey of life. After the crisis is over, we can and should enjoy life in the blessing and provision of Almighty God. Most of us would fall back into our routines and begin to assume smooth sailing from here on out. We would relax and believe the storm is over. All is well.

The Whole Creation Groans for Freedom

But then the cancer returns or the company lays everybody off or the widow's son dies. Alas, we do not live in a perfect world. We live in a chaotic, fallen world. *"We know that the whole creation has been groaning as in the pains of childbirth right up to the present time."*[1] Sin and rebellion against God is the ultimate explanation for all the human suffering, death, earthquakes, hurricanes, floods and wars that cause so much trouble. The whole creation groans to be set free from this terrible fallen state. But God is good all the time and there is victory in Jesus, even over the power of death, which is often misunderstood.

Sometimes, things need to die.

Death is the Restorative for the Human Condition

Death acts as the great restorative for the human condition and the natural realm. Indeed, life receives benefit from death in terms of evolution and sustenance. Jesus said, *"Unless a kernel of wheat falls to the ground and dies, it remains only a single seed. But if it dies, it produces many seeds."*2 Its death would release the power to multiply one seed into many, producing a great harvest. This is the miracle of Jesus Christ: the seed cannot be glorified unless it dies. The death and resurrection of Christ released the glory of eternal life to millions who believed the Gospel. To paraphrase the mighty Apostle Paul, *"To be dead to sin is to be alive to God in Christ Jesus."*3 It can be said that a higher form of spiritual existence is obtained only through the extinction of the lower form that preceded it.

The Body of Christ Revived will Become the Army of God

In the coming revival, the American church will enter a new paradigm of understanding bathed in prophetic revelation. Old understandings will pass away as the Spirit of God illuminates deeper understandings in a fresh outlook. The Apostle Paul declared, *"...no eye has seen, no ear has heard, no heart has imagined, what God has prepared for those who love Him. But God has revealed it to us by His Spirit. The Spirit searches all things, even the deep things of God.*"4 Thus enlightened, the body of Christ, revived as the Army of God, will make war on the kingdom of darkness. To facilitate this change, the Holy Spirit will empower believers to live by the *proceeding* word of the Lord.

The Proceeding Word of the Lord

Jesus declared, *"It is written, Man shall not live by bread alone, but by every word that proceedeth out of the mouth of God.*"5 A proceeding word issues forth and bubbles up from the place of origin – the mouth of God. It arises from the creative source of all things. Like springs of living water, Scripture comes alive in fresh revelation, out of the mouths of prophets.

From the Greek, this speaks of the *rhema* word of the Lord. Rhema is more than the inspired Scriptures, but also that strategic, permeating and revelatory word that dynamically alters the course of a believer's life. Hell's minions cannot withstand the power of the proceeding word. This is because it is a *confirming* word. The prophetic realm serves to help confirm the word of the Lord and comfort the church. It helps to establish what God has *already* spoken into our lives. The proceeding word of the Lord helps us prove the truth of all we are hearing. It transforms our doubts into faith. It revives us. It brings dead things back to life.

Elijah lived by the proceeding word of God and brought a dead child back to life.

The Death of the Widow's Son

After the nightmare existence she had already suffered through, the widow of Zarephath was dealt an even greater blow when her beloved son died from a sudden illness. Utterly heartbroken, she vented her emotions on Elijah and questioned him as to the cause of this calamity. In response, Elijah gently asked for the child and carried him up into the prophet's loft and laid him on the bed. Then, the prophet prayed, *"LORD my God, have you brought tragedy even on this widow I am staying with, by causing her son to die?"*6

The First Record of Raising the Dead in the Old Testament

The Scriptures indicate that Elijah stretched himself out on the boy three times and cried, *"Lord my God, let this* *boy's life return to him."*7 Then, the boy's life came into him again and Elijah brought the child down from the upper loft of the house and gave him to his astonished mother. And the widow said to Elijah, *"Now I know that you are a man of God and that the word of the Lord from your mouth is truth."*8

Interestingly, this was the first recorded miracle of raising the dead in the Old Testament. It was thought-provoking and raised certain questions: Was the child really dead or merely in a coma? Why did Elijah stretch himself three times over the boy's body? What purpose did this sudden death serve?

The answers are profound.

The Child was Actually Dead

First, the child was actually dead because the Scriptures declare that *"that there was no breath left in him."*9 Even comatose, there would still be breath. Without breath, there is death. When God made Adam, He breathed the *"breath of life"* into him and Adam became *"a living soul."*10 The Psalmist wrote, *"When his breath departs, he returns to the ground..."*11 In one moment, the child was without breath and dead. In another, his *"breath"* came back into him and he was alive.12 Without a genuine death, there could have been no miracle and no point for this event.

The Signature of the Godhead

Next, Elijah stretched himself three times upon the child's body. Some have speculated this may have been a healing ritual common to that time period. Elijah wanted to impart life from his own body to the lifeless body of the child. It was the power of prayer that persuaded the Almighty to give life to the boy, but Elijah worked with what he had – and that may have been to follow the techniques of the time. An alternative view has held that three is the number and signature of the Godhead – Father, Son and Holy Ghost. Thus, the three-fold act was tantamount to calling upon the name of Jehovah in the old covenant.

Finally, what purpose did the sudden death of this child really serve?

Elijah Did Not Always Know What God was Doing

First, it caused Elijah to inquire of God, *"Will you bring calamity upon this widow whose guest I am, and let her son die?"*13 This question provides evidence that Elijah did not *always* know in advance what God was doing. Also, tradition may have come into play again. Ancient custom instructed that if someone opened his house to you, then you were responsible for that person's well-being. Thus, Elijah was committed to save the lives of his hosts from both famine and death.

The Widow's Son and Jonah the Prophet

Next, according to rabbinical legend, a man named Amittai came from the tribe of Zebulon and lived at Zarephath. The legend held that the widow of Zarephath was the wife of Amittai and their child, whom Elijah raised from the dead, was to become Jonah the prophet. This explanation may be little more than a myth, but an interesting one nonetheless because it focuses on what *became* of the boy.

Elijah was Trained for His Next Supernatural Battle

Finally, the most provocative answer for the sudden death of the child may have nothing to do with the boy or the widow, *but everything to do with Elijah's faith*. This was God's training method for turning Elijah into a special forces warrior ready for the next battle. God was expanding Elijah's faith and preparing the prophet for the next huge confrontation with the demonic realm. If the prophet could not believe God to raise the dead, how would he have the courage to stand before hundreds of enemies and by faith, call down fire from heaven?

Sometimes, God needs to help increase our faith by allowing us to walk through hell so we can reach the blessings of heaven. The widow's son had to *die* to prove God's power over death, not simply sickness. In this way, God truly received great glory and Elijah entered a higher, more powerful dimension of faith.

Now watch this.

America Hurled Across the Threshold of Destiny

America, like the widow's son, has become sick unto death. Our nation has been hurled across the threshold of destiny into a dangerous new era of supernatural proportions. The national uproar of the year 2020 will pale in comparison to what is about to happen next.

A Prophetic Glimpse of Future Events

A series of disastrous diplomatic policies will ensue that can bring harm to the nation of Israel. Even though

Joe Biden promised on the campaign trail to keep the US Embassy in Jerusalem (if elected), he also stated at a virtual fundraiser in 2020, that the decision to move the embassy from Tel Aviv by President Donald Trump was "short-sighted and frivolous." However, believers should pay close attention to the Biden regime's evolving attitude toward our friends in Israel. In the future, Biden may become a "troubler of Israel." Further, voices in the Biden regime could begin to favor the removal of the US Embassy from the city of Jerusalem. Why? The supernatural key to America's success has always been our loving support of God's chosen people – Israel. The Psalmist declares, *"Pray for the peace of Jerusalem: they shall prosper that love thee."*14 However, Satan hates Jerusalem and the nation of Israel, the seat of the history, genealogy and future throne of King Jesus. It is that simple.

However, wrong-hearted presidents and wrong-headed diplomats will not stop what God is capable of doing next.

As God once looked upon Israel and Judah, He will cast His bright light upon America and command His spiritual armies: *"Should I not punish them for this?" declares the LORD. "Should I not avenge myself on such a nation as this? Go through her vineyards and ravage them, but do not destroy them completely. Strip off her branches, for these people do not belong to the LORD."*15

The lives of many will be ravaged by their refusal to believe that God will be so strict as His Word says He will. This is the same Satanic lie told to Eve in the garden of Eden which resulted in the fall of man. God always keeps His Word, even to the detriment of those who refuse to believe Him.

The Word of God will Explode in Power

A great supernatural awakening is coming and God will again prove Himself to America. In this environment, believers will live and flourish in the ways and means of the Lord. Faith will become substance. The Word of God will explode in power in heretofore unknown "Elijah" ministries. Only the Word of God, illuminated by prophetic revelation, can provide explanation and guidance for what comes next.

God will Strip Evil off the Branches in America

Soon, we shall be witnesses to His mighty works. God will strip evil off the branches in America. Satan's forces will rage. Strange weather events may wreak havoc on agricultural production in America's farm belt. Food distribution could be disrupted causing delivery and shortage issues.

Water system disruptions may occur in a large city. The spirits of fear and insanity will reign over certain metropolitan cities. Many in law enforcement will resign or retire in the midst of an anti-police climate, creating a vacuum that will attract lawless spirits. It will begin to seem as though America is falling. Many will lose hope.

The Army of God Declares War on the Kingdom of Darkness

But, in the midst of America's spiritual struggle, a holy remnant of true believers will arise, transformed as the Army of God, to declare war on the kingdom of darkness and defend the liberty of God in America. Enlightened believers will rejoice in the power of God in spite of failing economies and governments and food shortages. Signs and wonders will confirm the Word of God. Thousands will be saved and healed.

Make no mistake, this book is not about fighting a flesh and blood, physical enemy. Rather, it is written to discuss the coming spiritual battle with the invisible kingdom of darkness in America – including Baalism and other such demonic forces. The gospel message will be preached outside the confines of church buildings and the truth will set men free. Thus, America will rise from its former weaknesses to a greater place in God.

In some ways, the coming revival awakening in America will resemble the Early Church of the New Testament.

American Believers will Resemble the Early Church

The Early Church experienced a great deal of suffering and pain. Enemies who hated their guts surrounded them. They were scourged, stoned, sawn asunder, slain with the sword, tempted and mocked. Travel was limited to bone-jarring donkey rides or on foot. Itinerant preachers wore thin moccasins or went bare-footed, while crossing hundreds of miles of burning sand, thorns and jagged rocks. They carried the miracle Gospel message to the hurting and the lost. Instead of expensive suits and shoes, they wandered the wasteland in sheepskins and goatskins. They were often destitute, afflicted and tormented. The Bible says the world was not worthy of them.

Why did they do it?

The answer is not complicated. Simply put, they had been given a revelation of the power of Almighty God. They had power over all the power of the enemy. They had the power to heal, to work miracles, to convince and to spread the Gospel message like wildfire. They lived and breathed in the supernatural realm – the invisible kingdom of God. They were not their own anymore. They had become the sons of God.

The Violent Take the Kingdom of Heaven by Force

Jesus said, *"And from the days of John the Baptist until now the kingdom of heaven suffers violence, and the violent take it by force."*16 In essence, the Master is saying that soon many will flock to be close to Him, to be instructed in the ways of His kingdom; and some, who were formerly evil people, will cast off their evil ways and aggressively pursue the kingdom of God because they are so set on enjoying the blessings of it.

In the coming *Elijah Awakening*, multitudes will turn from their wicked ways and clamor for salvation. God is seeking men and women who will take the responsibility for revival upon their shoulders. In this way, America will literally be raised from the dead to walk in the light of God again.

CHAPTER SEVEN

Calling Down Fire on the Altar

ELIJAH MIRACLE 5

"Answer me, LORD, answer me, so these people will know that you, LORD, are God, and that you are turning their hearts back again. Then the fire of the LORD fell and burned up the sacrifice, the wood, the stones and the soil, and also licked up the water in the trench." 1 Kings 18:37-38 KJV

Elected American radicals and their wild-eyed constituencies have stupidly declared war on Almighty God by embracing Jezebel's agenda. Apostasy is rebellion against God because it is rebellion against truth. When apostasy reaches "critical mass," only delusional people assume God will have no reaction. In the time of Jezebel, Israel reached critical mass through the sexual deviancy and human sacrifice of Baal worship. To save them from this terrible apostasy, God first sent the drought and famine. Still, Israel continued in their sin. So, God decided to change His tactics. This time, He sent the prophet Elijah to call down the fire.

God Sends Elijah to Confront Ahab a Second Time

During the third year of drought, Elijah knew that it was causing catastrophic loss in the whole land. Men and beasts were devastated. All agricultural enterprise had burned up. Because Elijah felt responsible for the drought, the suffering and death of thousands of men, women and children greatly stirred his compassion and his conscience. Finally, Elijah could take it no more and prayed for the Lord to send rain. The Lord heard Elijah and quickly responded with a new twist, *"...Go and present yourself to Ahab, and I will send rain on the land..."* 1 So, Elijah left the widow's hideout in Zarephath and began the arduous journey to the northern kingdom of Israel to confront the King.

Surely Elijah walked by faith on the dusty trail to Samaria and trusted God to protect him from assassination. In fact, danger lurked everywhere for *any* person in service to God. Jezebel was actively hunting and slaughtering the prophets of Jehovah. The followers of Baal continued to persecute those who were faithful to Jehovah. The priests and Levites had fled into the southern kingdom of Judah and there was no public worship of Jehovah allowed in Israel. Because of this spiritual rebellion, a supernatural shadow of darkness had been cast over the land.

Fast forward to present-day America.

The Biden Regime has Crossed the Rubicon into Apostasy

A supernatural shadow of darkness has been cast over America. The Biden regime, joined by assorted lunatics in Congress and an array of alphabet agency bureaucrats, babbling nonsense, have likely crossed the Rubicon into apostasy. It appears they have determined that America will no longer be governed by the laws of God. Instead, they arouse and gratify the demons of Baal with their vigorous support for legal child sacrifice (abortion rights), laws favoring sexual deviancy that give LGBTQ+ values supremacy over heterosexual values and prohibit discrimination based on sexual orientation and gender identity. They aspire to teach sexual deviancy to America's children. They want to transform any preference for traditional sexual morality into actionable "hate," thus allowing lawsuits for all sorts of "discrimination," according to them.

Once this line was crossed, a heavenly stop watch began ticking and all bets were off. Almighty God will now be the final arbiter to decide when the stench of apostasy has reached critical mass. Nothing except repentance can stop what comes next.

In perspective, it is important to understand that God would have spared Sodom and Gomorrah if only ten righteous people could have been found. In the days of Jezebel, it is likely God spared Israel because there were some seven thousand faithful who had not bowed to Baal. In America, there are millions of us who faithfully love God and refuse to bow to Baal.

Something Huge is About to Happen in America

Millions of patriots have fasted and prayed earnestly for God to intervene in America's affairs. Marvelously, the Lord has *already set in motion* heavenly resources for the good of those who love Him. Thus, we must be remain faithful and wait upon the timing of God for what will happen next. Indeed, something is coming and, to quote our 45th President, Donald J. Trump: *"It's gonna be huge!"*

But first, we must return to ancient Israel.

When Elijah was en route to Samaria, King Ahab ordered the governor of his house, Obadiah, to venture out into the land seeking streams and brooks to find grass to feed their horses and mules. Ahab sent Obadiah in one direction and Ahab went another.

Ahab Looked for Grass Instead of Grace

Ahab was both evil and foolish. He could have resolved the crisis in Israel by repenting of his sin and leading his nation back to God. Yet he only fretted over the royal horses and mules. Instead of finding God's grace, Ahab looked for grass.

Obadiah, on the other hand, looked for grass and found Elijah. He fell on his face and said, *"Art thou that my lord Elijah?"* Elijah replied, *"I am: go tell thy lord, Behold Elijah is here."*2 Interestingly, this dialogue struck great fear in the heart of Obadiah.

The scriptures record that Obadiah feared the God of Israel and that when Jezebel began killing the prophets, Obadiah helped one hundred prophets of Jehovah to find hiding places in caves. There he fed them with bread and water. This took great courage and conviction to accomplish.

However, when Elijah commanded Obadiah to report to Ahab that Elijah had come to see him, Obadiah nearly fainted with fear. He argued that as soon as he went to Ahab, Elijah would probably be ordered by God to another location, causing Ahab to miss meeting Elijah and then punish Obadiah by killing him. This went back and forth, until Elijah promised Obadiah that he would indeed meet with Ahab. So Obadiah went to inform Ahab and the scriptures note that Ahab immediately went to meet Elijah.

Elijah the Troubler of Israel

At first sight, Ahab arrogantly accused Elijah, *"Is that you, you troubler of Israel?"*3 When righteousness stands its ground, evil always accuses it of wrongdoing. Elijah stood his ground and calmly responded, *"I have not made trouble for Israel, but you and your father's family have. You have abandoned the LORD's commands and have followed the Baals."*4 The tension between these two must have been thick enough to cut with a knife.

Evil Ahab blamed the prophet for the terrible conditions in Israel and likely wanted to murder Elijah. If Jezebel had been present, she would have tried to kill him. But, Jezebel was not there and Ahab was terrified of the anointed young prophet. The supernatural power and anointing of

Almighty God emanated from Elijah's person and the sinful monarch could literally feel it. He knew Elijah held the power of Jehovah and of the rain itself. So, Ahab kept his treacherous thoughts to himself.

Elijah Stood Alone Against 450 Prophets of Baal

With God's hand on his shoulder, Elijah feared neither man nor devil. Certainly, he did not fear the feckless Ahab. In fact, he treated the king like a servant and gave him the following commands: *"Now summon the people from all over Israel to meet me on Mount Carmel. And bring the four hundred and fifty prophets of Baal and the four hundred prophets of Asherah, who eat at Jezebel's table."*5 So it was that Ahab sent word throughout the land and gathered the prophets together on Mount Carmel.

When the appointed day came, thousands of people gathered on Mount Carmel. Ahab stood with the eight hundred and fifty prophets of Baal and Asherah. They held smoking censers and were costumed in elaborate robes. Elijah, the young prophet of God wore a camel's hair garment with a wide leather belt and he stood alone.

At some point, Elijah walked out to face the people and said, *"How long will you waver between two opinions?*

*If the Lord is God, follow him; but if Baal is God, follow him..."*6 But the people were only silent.

The God Who Answered by Fire

Then Elijah said to them, *"I am the only one of the Lord's prophets left, but Baal has four hundred and fifty prophets. Get two bulls for us. Let them choose one for themselves, and let them cut it into pieces and put it on the wood but not set fire to it. I will prepare the other bull and put it on the wood but not set fire to it. Then you call on the name of your god, and I will call on the name of the Lord. The god who answers by fire, he is God."*7 Then, the people voiced their agreement.

It should be noted that the four hundred and fifty prophets of Baal could not back out of this contest, lest the people would realize their impotence and deceit and stone them. Thus, they slaughtered the bull given to them and prepared it on the altar as instructed by Elijah and began calling on the name of Baal from morning until noon. They shouted, *"O Baal, answer us!"* But there was no response; Baal did not answer. So, these pagans danced around the altar they made. They moaned and screamed and leaped upon the altar in their desperation.

Elijah Mocks the Wicked Prophets of Baal

When the sun was directly overhead at noon, Elijah mocked them. He hollered at them, *"Shout louder!"* he said. *"Surely he is a god! Perhaps he is deep in thought, or busy, or traveling. Maybe he is sleeping and must be awakened."* 8 The sweating prophets of Baal fell into a frenzy – dancing, moaning, shouting loudly and leaping into the air. Desperate to engage Baal, they grew wilder and began cutting themselves with swords and spears until their blood flowed freely. The day dragged on as they continued their frantic activity until the time for the evening sacrifice. Still there was no response from Baal. His false prophets were exhausted. Nothing happened and no fire fell.

Elijah Rebuilds the Altar of God

Then Elijah called the people to come near him while he repaired the altar of the Lord that was broken down. He rebuilt it with twelve stones, according to the number of the tribes of the sons of Jacob. Then, Elijah dug a trench around the altar deep enough to hold about four gallons. He arranged wood on it and cut the bull into pieces that were placed on the wood. Next, the prophet ordered four barrels to be filled with water. This amount was dumped over the whole sacrifice and altar. Then they filled and dumped the barrels a second time and again, a third time, until the water ran around the altar and filled the trench.

At this point, things got interesting.

The sun was setting when Elijah collected himself and stepped forward. The Bible records that *"he came near."*9 This means he was putting some safe distance between himself and the altar area where a fiery explosion was about to occur. Please note the prophets of Baal did not do this. In their desperation and panic, they actually jumped all over their altar while they screamed and chanted. Elijah did none of those things.

Elijah Prays for God to Prove Himself

Instead, Elijah prayed a simple request, *"LORD, the God of Abraham, Isaac and Israel, let it be known today that you are God in Israel and that I am your servant and have done all these things at your command. Answer me, LORD, answer me, so these people will know that you, LORD, are God, and that you are turning their hearts back again."*9

Then, time and space seemed to distort.

The Fire of God Explodes

The atmosphere on Mount Carmel suddenly changed. The air grew dense and heavy. Suddenly, out of the invisible ether, the fire of God exploded upon the altar like a nuclear blast. The heat was so extreme it consumed the meat sacrifice, the wood and even, the stones!

Interestingly, it is likely the stones used for the altar were of sandstone. The melting point of sandstone is approximately 2,380 degrees Fahrenheit. However, to consume these materials, it would take hours at this temperature. On the other hand, lightning measures about 54,000 Fahrenheit (more than 5 times the surface temperature of the sun). In other words, at the temperature of lightning, it would only take several seconds to atomize Elijah's sacrifice and altar. Did God use lightning to accomplish His purposes? No one knows and no one cares. The point is: God proved Himself to be the One True God in a spectacular manner that could not be refuted!

No one said a word. An eerie silence blanketed the area. Nothing but the smell of ozone and a soot haze lingered over the blackened area, now slightly hollowed out, where the altar once stood. Suddenly, Ahab, his false prophets and the thousands of Israelites who witnessed this phenomenon, fell on their faces as if they were poleaxed and cried, *"The LORD, He is God; the LORD, He is God!"*10

Elijah Executes the Prophets of Baal

While prostrate on the ground, the thoroughly terrified King Ahab and his evil prophets began to wonder how they were going to make it safely back down the mountain. They were the leading perpetrators of Baalism in Israel and they were without excuse. They had consorted with demons and were caught red-handed by God. They now desperately hoped the show was over. But God was not finished with them. A terrible price was yet to be paid for the particularly insidious apostasy of Baalism.

All were lying on the ground in terror, except Elijah – the last man standing. The prophet turned to them with a steely gaze and said, *"Seize the prophets of Baal. Don't let anyone get away!"*11 The people grabbed the frightened prophets and Elijah had them dragged down to the Kishon Valley where they were summarily slaughtered by the sword.11 It is possible that Elijah did the killing himself.12 Either way, there was a purpose for this execution.

This ruthless slaughter of Baal's prophets was the culmination of the fierce righteousness and anointing of Elijah and the spirit of the old law. Under the express command of the Law, those who committed idolatry were to be put to death. Elijah, by the theocratic right of a prophet of God, could step in and execute the Law when the king failed in his duty. Besides, who there would argue with him?

So, Elijah seized the moment to require the people to rise up and demonstrate their conviction with action, regardless of whether their actions would expose them to the anger of King Ahab or Queen Jezebel. Elijah knew that if they committed themselves to this execution, their bonds to Baal would be forever broken. And God was watching.

Further, Elijah had these evil prophets frog-marched down into the nearly dry Kishon ravine to meet their end. It has been speculated that this was done to leave the bodies in a place where they could not be found. Elijah knew the rains were coming and floodwaters would soon roar through the Kishon ravine, sweeping the bodies out to sea.

God is a Nationalist but the Antichrist is a Globalist

In America, the rogue Biden regime and leftist Democrats have seemingly mounted a war against God. Apparently, they seek to rebuild the Tower of Babel. This insanity has evolved through years of plotting and scheming. Now, the United States of America, like ancient Israel, is torn between two opinions.

On one side of the divide, millions of all races still love the God of the Bible and American nationalism. God has proven His preference for nationalism with the nation of Israel – His chosen people. On the other side, there are those who promote the agenda of Jezebel and Luciferian globalism – the new world order of the Antichrist.

God proved His opposition to globalism when all men spoke one language and the Tower of Babel was planned. Evil men plotted to build a city and a tower reaching into the heavens to make a name for themselves. This was a snapshot of the mind of Lucifer when he rebelled against God and sought to seat himself on the throne of God. He wanted to ascend into heaven and make a name for himself – to be like the Most High God.13 The Lord destroyed this satanic effort on the earth when He confused their one language into many and scattered them abroad over the face of the earth.14

Then, there are the phlegmatic RINOs who lurk in the corners. These are the weak sisters who want to have it both ways. In this, they resemble the tainted Judas Iscariot who claimed to follow Jesus, but loved thirty pieces of silver a lot more. Brother Judas (and his sticky fingers) was the keeper of the bag containing Jesus' ministry money. Judas loved money and his position in the group, but not Jesus. Judas loved the wrong things. RINOs can often resemble Judas because they love the wrong things (globalism and warmongering), while they wave tiny American flags. However, Jesus said, *"No one can serve two masters. Either you will hate the one and love the other, or you will be devoted to the one and despise the other..."*15

This explains why globalists can't see the forest for the trees – they claim to love America, but seek to subordinate American interests in order to promote the Antichrist agenda of a globalist, new world order. They love endless wars, not peace. Some RINOs even favor giving offerings to Baal – using American tax dollars to pay for abortions. Sometimes, they wear the mask of Christianity, but in reality, they are servants to the spirit of the world and not the Spirit of God. They may praise Jehovah in public like Pharisees, but secretly bow to Baal.

A brilliant man once said, "Three traitors inside the garrison may do it more harm than three thousand who lay siege against it from the outside." For many years, these "inside the garrison" types have done more harm to America and the cause of God than we imagined – anything that siphons off the national unity and faith in God is the work of the kingdom of darkness. Period. There is no other explanation.

The Fire of God Will Fall in America

Soon, the *Elijah Awakening* will electrify Americans to pray for the fire of God to fall on the altar again. At Mount Carmel, the supremacy of the Living God was established over the power of the enemy. This is about to happen in America.

Consider "the fire of God" in spiritual terms.

The Elijah anointing always precedes the fire of God and the drastic changes it produces. John the Baptist was the New Testament gold standard for this phenomenon. He said, *"The ax is already at the root of the trees, and every tree that does not produce good fruit will be cut down and thrown into the fire. I baptize you with water for repentance. But after me comes one who is more powerful than I, whose sandals I am not worthy to carry. He will baptize you with the Holy Spirit and fire. His winnowing fork is in his hand, and he will clear his threshing floor, gathering his wheat into the barn and burning up the chaff with unquenchable fire."*16

God and Fire Cannot be Separated

God and fire cannot be separated. The Bible declares, *"Our God is a consuming fire."*17 The sudden appearance of fire fills scripture after scripture. When David offered a sacrifice to the Lord, fire descended from heaven and consumed it. Elijah called down heavenly fire that vaporized wood, stone and water. Later, he was swept by whirlwind into heaven at the appearance of a chariot and horses of fire. At the end of Solomon's prayer, fire fell from heaven upon his altar. Elisha made a fire. Micah prophesied fire. Jesus said, *"I am come to bring fire on the earth."*18 John the Baptist promised Christ would baptize us with fire. Without His fire, we can never demonstrate His power.

The power of God flows after the process of spiritual alignment has occurred. Jesus declared, *"But ye shall receive power, after that the Holy Ghost is come upon you..."*19 The power arrives *after* the Holy Ghost comes upon you. Something happens *after* and many believers in America do not know what it is.

The Power of God Comes After the fire

The power only comes after the fire aligns us with God's purpose. For years, many in the church assumed that the baptism of fire is an experience of joy and wild excitement. To be sure, fire does snap, crackle and pop. But joy and excitement are not found in close proximity to fire. The inherent nature of God's holy fire produces something supernatural in the human being. It causes us to know without doubt that God is God – the Alpha and the Omega, the beginning and the end. It unburdens us from ourselves and puts us in spiritual order.

The Fire of God Burns What We Don't Need

Holy Ghost fire burns temporal things. It separates the precious things of God from the vile. It will burn our worldly flesh and it causes great pain when it does. The Bible says that Jesus will remove the garbage in our lives with an unquenchable fire. God knows how much heat is needed in our lives to bring us into His purpose. He will not burn our seed, but He will only burn up the chaff that has managed to infiltrate our lives. Chaff is the husk of the wheat. It is the temporal matter – the worldly things we don't need. When the fire falls on our altar, it burns them up.

How God picks Leaders in the Elijah Awakening

In the *Elijah Awakening*, God will pick His leaders from the fires of holocaust. They will be hurting, wounded and healed people who have been baptized with fire on the firing line of faith. God will pick those who have been tried and tested in the fire of battle. Why? Because in God's kingdom, battle scars are not undesirable. They are the prerequisites to power.

When God looks for leaders in the coming awakening, He will look for scars. This is because scars are badges of honor. Jesus sees Himself when He sees scars. When the mighty Commander of heaven's armies reaches for another recruit, He reaches with hands that were deeply scarred by the bloody nails of Calvary's crucifixion, the supreme conflict. God picks warriors cast in His image, plucked from the Refiner's fire.

Battles are not won by soldiers who have never fired a shot or torn down a dark stronghold. Battle are won by those who will confront the kingdom of darkness where it lives. God seeks captains like Joshua and David who will invade the enemy's territory in the power of His Word. He searches for those who will confront evil where it lives.

Jesus was the ultimate confronter. He was manifested to destroy the kingdom of darkness and crush the head of the serpent. He is king of kings and Lord of Lords. Through Jesus' leadership, we are more than conquerors. We will run the race and not be weary. We will walk many miles and not faint.

And in the coming days of the *Elijah Awakening*, this is precisely how we will take America back for the glory of God.

Patriots must begin to pray: Dear Lord, let the fire of God fall in America.

CHAPTER EIGHT

Calling Down the Rain

ELIJAH MIRACLE 6

"And Elijah said unto Ahab, Get thee up, eat and drink; for there is a sound of abundance of rain." 1 Kings 18:41 KJV

The rain of God is coming to help American believers and we need to get ready for it. God is saying, *"For I will pour water on the thirsty land, and streams on the dry ground; I will pour out my Spirit on your offspring, and my blessing on your descendants."*1 The outpouring of heavenly water will wash away the corruption from the crack house to the White House. It will cleanse the land of the doctrines of devils that have ruined our schools, colleges, governments and media. But, those devils cannot dodge

133

much longer. God is sending the rain to end the drought in America's soul. We will be transformed by rivers of living water. Nothing can stop the power of mighty rivers in the storm season and the clouds are already gathering.

The Revival of the Third Day is Coming

All across the fruited plain, the Lord has heard the fervent prayers of believers and He is about to pour out a "latter rain" spiritual event on America (see my previous work called *The Third Day*). It will be as the lightning flashes from East to West; it will be witnessed by many, all at once. There is nothing devils or the radical Left can do to stop this move of God.

In the Bible, rain is a type of the outpouring of the Holy Spirit. The Psalmist said, *"He shall come down like rain… as showers that water the earth."*2 The Lord declared, *"Drop down, ye heavens, from above, and let the skies pour down righteousness…"*3 He promised us, *"… I will cause the shower to come down in his season; there shall be showers of blessing."*4 Hosea prophesied of this mighty *Third Day* revival saying, *"Come and let us return to the Lord: … after two days will He revive us: in the third day He will raise us up, … He shall come unto us as the rain…"* 5 Jesus said, *"Whoever believes in me, as Scripture has said, rivers of living* *water will flow from within them.* "6 Soon, the Holy Spirit will explode on us to overcome all the power of the enemy.

Demons Do Not Like Water

Demonic entities do not like water. Jesus said, *"When the unclean spirit is gone out of a man, he walketh through dry places, seeking rest..."* 7 Unclean spirits (demons) roam about in dry places, where there is no water. The New American Standard translates dry places as waterless places. And the *"rest"* the demon seeks refers to demonic possession of a human. The *"dry places"* refer to sinners who have no living water. Those who lack the indwelling of the Holy Spirit are prime targets. Those who worship Baal and promote the Jezebel Agenda fit this profile. They cannot stand the rain of God.

New Prophetic Voices will Shake the Foundations of Hell

When this revival rain begins to fall, God will anoint prophetic warriors (the *Elijah Awakening*) with exciting spiritual gifts to actualize their primary assignment to make war on the Jezebel Agenda in America. This war will not be won by Godless politicians, but by the Spirit of the Lord.

New prophetic voices will shake the foundations of hell to edify, exhort and comfort American believers. They will have the mind of Christ to help clarify and magnify their efforts. The mind of Christ provides a conscious connection to the source of all power in heaven and in earth – God the Father.

Elijah had a serious conscious connection with God the Father.

God told Elijah that He Would Send the Rain

Before the prophet departed the widow's home in Zarephath, he knew the rain was going to fall again. God had already told him: *"Go shew thyself unto Ahab; and I will send rain upon the earth."* 8 After the miracle of three and half years of a burning drought, God was about to perform another miracle to release the rain.

Rain falls when God decides it should fall. During the flood of Noah, it was used once for judgment and punishment. But God promised never to flood the earth in that way again. In Elijah's day, God withheld the rain to bring Israel into alignment with His purposes. For three and half years, the land burned up in the drought. Thousands starved in the resulting famine. God did not do these things because He is mean. He did these things to draw them away from the demonic worship of Baal.

At this time, Elijah had just orchestrated the explosive events on Mount Carmel. He had just finished calling fire down from heaven and putting a bloody sword to the four hundred and fifty prophets of Baal in the Kishon Valley near the base of the mountain. Upon returning, Elijah walked up to fearful Ahab and told him to go celebrate (*"eat and drink"*) for the sound of rain was in the air.

Ahab Celebrated, but Elijah Prayed for Rain

In this, King Ahab was not a man to argue. After he witnessed the fire fall on the altar of God at Elijah's word, the king was far too traumatized to disregard Elijah. So he quickly set about to celebrate the promise of rain. But Elijah did not join in the festivities. Instead, he took his servant and climbed to the summit of Mount Carmel. There, Elijah bent down and put his face between his knees to pray.9

On the mountaintop, Elijah's prayer has a pattern that patriots can use in the war for the soul of America.

Miracle Prayer is Based on the Promise of God

First, Elijah based his miracle prayer for rain on the stated promise of God: *"I will send rain upon the earth."*10 The Bible declares it was God's will to send the rain. Why then did Elijah need to pray for rain? The answer is that God loves to use human agency to accomplish His purposes on the earth. God created human beings as free moral agents and He is joyful when we freely choose to serve Him. Therefore, while it was already the will of God to send rain, He required somebody to pray for the rain before it would happen. Jesus said, *"You may ask me for anything in my name, and I will do it."*11 The promises of God are ready and waiting for us in heaven. It is up to us to pull them into the earthly realm by the prayer of faith.

Miracle Prayer is Done in Secret

Next, Elijah prayed in a secret, quiet place, away from the madding crowd. Ahab celebrated with eating and drinking, but Elijah separated himself from that sideshow. He prayed alone on the mountaintop. There is a powerful method here. Jesus prayed alone on the mountainside. 12 Jesus said, *"But when you pray, go into your room, close the door and pray to your Father, who is unseen. Then your*

Father, who sees what is done in secret, will reward you."13 While radicals and devils run amok in our streets, we must find a quiet place to seek the Lord for America.

Miracle Prayer seeks a Specific Outcome

Next, Elijah prayed for a specific outcome. He did not ask God for three things. He asked for one thing – rain. The Apostle Paul did not focus on several objectives in His ministry. He said, "*… but this one thing I do…*"14 Paul pressed toward the mark! Believers in America should desire one thing right now – a spiritual realignment with God. Like Elijah, we need to pray for the rain. Once this begins, everything else will fall into place.

Pray and Wait for the Miracle Answer

Finally, Elijah watched and prayed *until the miracle appeared.* The Bible account shows that God did not immediately respond, but Elijah was determined. The Psalmist said, "*I waited patiently for the LORD; he turned to me and heard my cry.*"15 Time and again, Elijah asked his servant to go and look at the sky (toward the sea) for signs of rain. Each time, the servant would report, "*There is nothing.*"16

Each time, Elijah would pray and evaluate the situation further.

American believers would do well to learn from this.

Not Everything can be Blamed on Donkeys or Elephants

The election of 2020 became a nightmare for the MAGA movement when it was widely alleged that Donald J. Trump lost because of a massive election fraud scheme. Of course, Democrats were flabbergasted and outraged that Republicans would suggest such a thing! Meanwhile, Bible-believing patriots everywhere have fallen into a controlled rage state. We have grown weary with the watered-down, pablum excuses we are force-fed by spineless RINOs at local, state and national levels and the radical insanity vomited from across the aisle. Indeed, the system appears to be hopelessly broken and beyond repair. However, not everything can be blamed solely on woke donkeys or flatulent elephants. The real source of our troubles is beyond the natural realm. Our true problem is rooted in the spiritual disability of our nation.

America is Starved for the Power of the Gospel

Frighteningly, America has become spiritually disabled as never before by the popular pulpit promotion of a weightless, sugar water form of godliness that cannot solve problems or overcome demonic oppression. Tragically, there are some standing behind sacred American pulpits who have no business there. The glorious Gospel of Christ can provide solid spiritual food for starving humans. But, instead of experiencing incredible joy and the glory of God, many today are weeping in a state of utter hopelessness because the anointed Word of the Lord is not preached to them. They are starved for the power of the risen Christ. Many sing and clap their hands, but deception, discouragement and divorce regularly walk the aisles of every house of worship. Some have fallen away in sheer disappointment.

The Biden Regime is a Nightmare with a Lousy Set of Facts

Since the floundering Biden regime took office, every day brings more of a demonic nightmare into focus. The government threatens our freedoms with mandatory vaccinations, masks and lockdowns. Our borders are out of control. Wild Marxists and other leftist thugs commit mayhem in the streets and no one stops them. Large cities have become dangerous, dry places favored by demons. Americans seek good news, but nothing good appears on our horizon. We are like Elijah on that mountaintop, praying for rain, but seeing no clouds. What a lousy set of facts!

But the truth is greater than a lousy set of facts. Truth is more powerful than the fake news media and their virtue signaling. Truth sets us free and the truth is: God has not finished with America!

The Rolling Thunder of Heaven will Signal God's People

The rolling thunder of heaven will signal God's people that the rain will fall. It will separate the precious from the vile. In this revival rain, the true American patriot will put God first and everything else second. Real people of faith will obey Him without a moment's hesitation. They will not need to be rocked in their cradle to be kept sanctified. Naysayers, bigots and riotous railers will find no place among God's people. The downpour will wash them away.

The rain of God will transform us into warriors. True believers are not ashamed of the Gospel or its miraculous power. They love the liberty of the Holy Spirit. They love not their lives, even unto death. Patrick Henry famously said, *"Give me liberty or give me death."* Money will not buy these Americans and they will refuse to become discouraged even when their best friends turn and walk away, God holds them firmly in the palm of His hand and no man or devil can pluck them out! We will win this fight because those who are with us are more than those who are with them!17

We need to take action in the supernatural realm.

From One Hand, Thousands of Helping Hands will Appear

We need to rise to our feet in expectation and watch and pray like Elijah. Something is about to happen for our good. The rain is coming. It may have small beginnings (the size of one man's hand), but it will flash across America like lightning! Soon, in the coming outpouring, thousands of helping hands will appear to join in the fight.

This is why Elijah prayed and evaluated and repeatedly sent his servant to observe the sky. Finally, the seventh time the servant reported, *"A cloud as small as a man's hand is rising from the sea."* So Elijah said, *"Go and tell Ahab, 'Hitch up your chariot and go down before the rain stops you.'"*18

Now watch this.

The Bible records that the *"heaven was black with clouds and wind, and there was a great rain. And Ahab rode, and went to Jezreel. And the hand of the Lord was on Elijah; and he girded up his loins, and ran before Ahab to the entrance of Jezreel."*19 The rain came just as God had promised! The drops began falling before they could get off the mountain.

Elijah and Apache Warriors in the American Southwest

At a height of less than 2000 feet above sea level, Mount Carmel would be considered a "great big hill" in Texas (just kidding). Still, it would take some time for scores of people to descend the dangerous slopes of the mountain and make their way on foot out onto the open plain in a blinding rain. Ahab and his men rolled along in chariots pulled by horses. But, Elijah, wearing rough garments and leather moccasins, *ran ahead of Ahab* to Jezreel. Read this as: *Elijah outran Ahab's horses* all the way to Jezreel. This was a distance of 15 to 20 miles.

What significance does this running feat hold?

Some believe this feat was another Elijah miracle. We know that God loved Elijah and helped him. While Elijah's running ahead of the horses was extraordinary, it does not actually rise to the miraculous. By comparison, the abil-

THE ELIJAH AWAKENING

ity of the Apache warrior in the American southwest was equally pronounced. They trained to run long distances in harsh terrain, blistering heat, with no water and no special footwear. It was said that an Apache warrior could run 50+ miles without stopping and travel more swiftly than a troop of mounted soldiers. Therefore, it can be stated that both Elijah and the Apaches were exceptional runners. Who in modern ministry could equal such a feat?

However, something else is going on here.

Emphasis on Elijah

Some scholars have placed emphasis on *Elijah*, theorizing that God's prophet was attempting to demonstrate his humility as a faithful subject of Ahab to soften the king's heart and bring him back to the Lord before he was again dragged down into sin by the influence of wicked Jezebel. However, this logic does not square with Elijah's stern personality, rigid resolve or his official status as a prophet of Jehovah under the Law. Thus, Elijah belonged to Almighty God and was not a faithful subject of evil Ahab. Sometimes, we must "*obey God rather than men.*"[20] Therefore, the idea that Elijah was a humble and faithful subject of Ahab simply does not compute.

145

Emphasis on Ahab

Another theory has placed the emphasis on *Ahab*.

If Ahab had paid the respect to Elijah that he deserved, he would have invited him into his chariot, to honor him before the elders of Israel and confer with him about the spiritual needs of the kingdom. But Ahab did not offer respect or kindness to the prophet of Almighty God. It must be remembered that Ahab was more evil and unrepentant than any other king before him. It was not in his sinful and arrogant nature to offer comfort to the man of God or seek his advice.

Emphasis on God

The best answer puts the emphasis where it belongs – on *God* and His kingdom business. In this, God does not need the help of kings. By extension, neither does His prophet.

Similarly, the church of Jesus Christ does not exist by the grace of the government. The church is victorious by the power of Almighty God. Further, God does not rule the universes by the charitable favors of petty tyrants. Thus, the man of God ran *ahead* of Ahab's chariots, not behind them. Elijah did not draw sustenance from a king, nor did he pay tribute to an enthroned mortal.

The American Revolutionary War was won by patriots because of such ideas.

Patriots Do Not Need a King

In spite of the current radical regime, American patriots do not need a king to offer them a chariot ride in exchange for their freedom. Our rights to life, liberty and the pursuit of happiness flow from heaven's portals and exist beyond the reach of any government's power. These rights are unalienable and endowed by our Creator. This conviction is in the DNA of every real, God-fearing American. Some of our own have died for these rights.

America was founded on the consent of the governed to allow their government to protect their God-given rights, not abolish them at the whim of a tyrant. When the government removes such rights and forces free men into a dependency on the government, America becomes Venezuela. Indeed, real Americans will never exchange their freedom for a ride on the king's chariot.

And so it was that Elijah ran to Jezreel with the hand of God on his shoulder and the rain on his face.

Jezreel, the site of Ahab's summer palace, was some 21 miles north of the capital city of Samaria. Within the walls of this palace, Jezebel anxiously awaited the king's return. She hoped to hear of the great victory won by the prophets of Baal. She must have paced the floors like a caged lioness waiting for the triumphant king. Instead, she got a rain soaked king with a wild story about falling fire and slashing swords and Elijah.

Jezebel and the Fake News

Ahab spun the story like a fake news report and made Elijah the centerpiece of the narrative.21 He blamed Elijah as if the prophet had somehow brought fire down from heaven on his own. He then told in bloody detail how Elijah had mercilessly slain all the prophets of Baal. Ahab never bothered to tell his tempestuous wife that Elijah had committed no crime and that the lives of these prophets were justly forfeited under the Law of God. He never tried to convince her to turn from Baal and worship Jehovah. He never mentioned one word about the miraculous rainstorm. Instead, evil Ahab purposely misconstrued the events at Mount Carmel to incite Jezebel's rage against Elijah. It was a royal setup.

And it worked like a charm.

Jezebel Sends a Death Threat to Elijah

True to form, Jezebel went berserk and sent a messenger to Elijah threatening, *"May the gods deal with me, be it ever so severely, if by this time tomorrow I do not make your life like that of one of them [the slain prophets of Baal]."* 22 It is likely the messenger found Elijah as he huddled near the city gate and informed him of Jezebel's great threat.

The message revealed that Jezebel dominated the king according to her own will. She did as she pleased. Further, it proved her arrogance – she ignored the significance of God's power on Mount Carmel and was more determined than ever to worship Baal.

Worse, she wanted to destroy Jehovah's prophet.

Elijah Runs for His Life and Falls into Depression

Thus, Elijah ran for his life. His hopes for the deliverance of Israel were shattered. He had just enough time to gather his cloak and his servant and leave. This time he made his way to the realm of King Jehoshaphat in the southern kingdom of God's people. When he came to Beersheba in Judah, he left his servant there and went on alone into the wilderness of Arabia. Alas, Elijah could not rest in Judah because Jehoshaphat was allied to Ahab and unable to offer sanctuary to Elijah.

So Elijah wearily continued on into the wilderness for a full day. The Scriptures declare, *"… He came to a broom bush, sat down under it and prayed that he might die. "I have had enough, LORD," he said. "Take my life; I am no better than my ancestors."* 23

Elijah thought he had done what God wanted. He had just prayed for rain to end the drought and God gave the rain – a miracle. He confronted the evil prophets of Baal and called fire down from heaven. He witnessed thousands of Israelites as they fell on their faces before God. He fearlessly executed the four hundred and fifty prophets of Baal. He even outpaced the chariots of the king all the way to Jezreel. But none of it mattered. Jezebel wanted to kill him and he just wanted to quit.

God Would Never Allow Jezebel to Kill Elijah

Please notice that Jezebel sent Elijah a message, instead of a royal hitman to kill him on the spot. She actually gave him a chance to run by first warning him with the message. Was this God's intervention in Elijah's moment of weakness? Of course, in the message, Jezebel swore her oath by gods that already were exposed as powerless. Elijah should have known there was nothing to fear from her demon gods. In fact, Satan himself could not kill Elijah, because only God holds the keys to death and life. Elijah should have known better than to believe the fake news from Jezebel's messenger.

While it is true that Jezebel murdered other "prophets" of Jehovah, none of them possessed the supernatural prophetic ability exhibited by Elijah and confirmed by God. Elijah was unique. The others were more akin to professional priests or academics. Elijah had not chosen to be a prophet as one would choose a profession. He had been hand picked by God and empowered for this task. He was utterly protected by God.

Therefore, Elijah was not in danger and he could have simply bedded down for the night. If God could rain fire down on the altar, He could certainly prevent Jezebel from harming Elijah. God had assigned Elijah to confront Ahab and Jezebel and turn Israel back to God. The Lord never wanted Elijah to wildly run into the wilderness of Arabia to sulk under juniper trees and hide in caves.

The Elijah Awakening will make America First

Soon, the *Elijah Awakening* will raise up thousands of spiritual warriors to confront the Jezebel Agenda and take our nation back for the glory of God. Just as Elijah was assigned to make Israel the "first priority" for the Lord's deliverance, America must now be our first priority. It is no secret that Christians love Israel and pray for the peace of Jerusalem. In fact, all gentile believers are considered *"spiritual Israel,"* grafted into the tree of God's chosen people, by our faith in Christ.24 Now, patriots must push the devil and his followers out of the way and make America our first priority again, just as our founders did. Otherwise, we will forfeit our country to the dark agenda of globalist wolves.

For too long, we have been cursed with spineless Washington swamp dwellers (RINOs, Democrats, entrenched leftist bureaucrats – the Uniparty) concerned with seeing and being seen at the next cocktail party. There is little question that leftist Democrats have likely lost their minds. However, we have also been thwarted by out-of-touch, obstructionist, warmongering, RINOs in the Senate and House, babbling about "civility" and their "friends across the aisle." Meanwhile, Jezebel burns cities to the ground and murders babies. Alas, there are no friends in the kingdom of darkness, only the enemies of God. Light cannot be joined to darkness. Today, you either stand with Jehovah or you stand with Satan. There is no "moderate" position. Elected officials who are blinded to this simple fact are on the wrong wavelength and they must be legally purged at the earliest opportunity. They do not represent God or His spiritual warriors.

The Army of God does not make friends among the minions of hell. We do not need to mingle in a Washington cocktail party. We are a spiritual *war party* that can fight devils and take America back from misbegotten thieves! We have the authority of God to war against powers, principalities and the rulers of darkness. The Bible declares there is a *"time of war..."*25 Now is the time for all good men and women to go to war against every devil in the Jezebel Agenda with Spirit-filled leaders that know how to fight.

God says Stand and Fight

Just now, Almighty God is saying to America, *"How long will you listen to lying spirits and fake news? You do not need to be afraid. I have never left you and I will never leave you. I am not finished with America. I am just getting started. When will you wake up and say, 'Enough of this foolishness!' Get out of the cave. It's time to take a stand, to fight back – to take control of your future!"*

The rain of God is coming to America and the spirit of Elijah will be upon us to make great changes. We must learn and prepare. It will soon be time to once again call down the fire of God to destroy the works of the enemy!

In light of this, we derive rules.

Rules of the Rain

Rule 1. *Rain unmasks demons because they need dry places to rest.* (Luke 11:24).

The Jezebel Agenda and Baalism serve and cooperate with entities from the dark kingdom of Lucifer (Satan). These entities seek dry places "to rest" (read: possess a new host). Rain is a type of the Holy Spirit and speaks to the outpouring of God's Spirit. Jesus told us that God sends rain to the just and the unjust. (Matthew 5:45). Demons are unjust spirits. Rain moves God's people to do great exploits, but rain whips demons into fear and frenzy. They were terrified of Jesus and ran screaming from His voice. Therefore, they are terrified of the Jesus in us. Thus, genuine revival will be opposed and punctuated by demonic activity. This opposition proves that we are "over the target" and winning.

Rule 2. *Do not enter enemy territory until God gives the order.* (Psalm 119:35).

When we consult the Lord, He will tell us when and where to go. Otherwise, we are asking for an ambush. Elijah broke this rule by running to Jezreel when God did not direct him there. This mistake may have exacerbated the death threat from Jezebel and Elijah's subsequent depression. In Jezreel, *he lost his faith and ran;* even though God's hand was on him. Elijah lost the "mind of Christ" and fell victim to the spirits of fear and confusion.

By contrast, when God told him to go to Zarephath in Jezebel's home territory, all things worked together for good and Elijah's faith was strengthened for the next battle. Remember, we are in a supernatural war and simply cannot not run ahead of God. It is too dangerous. Devils and lefty lunatics are on every hand hoping for a chance to hurt us. It is imperative that we follow God's lead in all things.

Rule 3. *Do not give place to fear.*

F.E.A.R. is False Evidence Appearing Real. Fear is a hindering spirit, but God has not given us the spirit of fear. He has given us power, love and self-discipline. (2 Timothy 3:7). God is not the author of confusion. (1 Corinthians

14:33). We cannot win this war if we react badly to the spirit of fear. The secret is to consult God before we act. Elijah only felt fear when he forgot all about God and the drought and the fire and the rain. He forgot everything God taught him in his special anointing and just ran like a man chased by goblins. But, fear wins only when we leave God out of the equation. *"Wherefore take unto you the whole armour of God, that ye may be able to withstand in the evil day, and having done all, to stand."* (Ephesians 6:13 KJV).

Rule 4. *Truth, not facts, will make us free.* (John 8:32).

We must walk by faith, not by sight. Fake news and lousy facts are stock-in-trade for Jezebel's agenda. Fake news facts can fool us. In Elijah's case, mistakes were made with facts. The facts were – Jezebel wanted to gut him like a fish; but the truth was – God would not allow it.

Sadly, Elijah ran from Jezebel when he believed the facts and forgot the truth. Yet, even in his mistakes, God never left Elijah and kept His hand upon him. As a result, the prophet lived to fight another day. God had his back. In this same way, God protects every American who loves Him and keeps His commandments. God's truth is more powerful than a lousy set of facts.

"You, dear children, are from God and have overcome them, because the one who is in you is greater than the one who is in the world." (1 John 4:4 NIV).

Take heart America, the rain is coming and the *Elijah Awakening* is coming with it!

CHAPTER NINE

Calling Down Fire on the Enemy

ELIJAH MIRACLE 7

"And Elijah answered and said to the captain of fifty, 'If I be a man of God, then let fire come down from heaven and consume thee and your fifty!' And there came down fire from heaven, and consumed him and his fifty.'" 2 Kings 1:10,12 KJV

Look no further than the Christian MAGA movement to be a landing zone for the *Elijah Awakening* when it arrives, to aid the people of God. In due time, they will be filled with power from on high to call down the fire of God on the Jezebel Agenda in America. From the church house to the townhouse to the farmhouse, men and women will be called of God to be modern "Elijahs" – powerful instruments for the cause of Christ to destroy the Jezebel Agenda in supernatural warfare. The Old Testament prophet Elijah was assigned to save Israel and the worship of Jehovah from being corrupted by the demonic religion of Baalism. Now, the spirit of Elijah will be raised up in America to confront Baalism cloaked in the robes of a Marxist revolution.

A caveat: While this chapter highlights another miracle by Elijah involving heavenly fire, there is something to be discovered beyond the fire. The events involving the explosion of fire, while breathtaking, are subordinate to the *confrontation* in the supernatural realm. The buried lead is that miraculous acts of God *follow* confrontation with evil.

Confrontation with Evil is Evidence of Faith

Confrontation with evil follows *faith* in God. Faith produces miracles. From another angle, it can be said that confrontation with evil is *evidence* of faith. It speaks of spiritual violence – only the violent take the prize by the force of faith. Throughout the ages, those who serve the Lord have confronted dark opposition with a violence of conviction and passion. They were unafraid of harsh circumstances or outcomes. They were not deterred by what bad men or devils said they could or could not do. In spite of many dangers, toils and snares, they refused to be driven away from the purposes of heaven in their lives. For generations, God has used people who know how to confront sin and use heaven's resources on the enemies of God.

Consider the confrontations that exploded in fire when Israel's new king stupidly decided to track down and arrest God's anointed prophet, Elijah.

King Ahab and Jezebel were the parents of King Ahaziah, who took the throne after Ahab was killed in battle. After his coronation, he continued the evil and perverse worship of Baal, following the same dark path as his wicked parents. Since Jezebel was alive during the reign of her son, her evil influence continued to permeate the land. Thus, God was once again provoked to anger by the actions of Israel's evil leadership.

King Ahaziah sent an Inquiry to Baalzebub

The second book of Kings records that Ahaziah suffered a grievous injury from a fall. Bible scholars have theorized that the upper chamber of his palace in Samaria had a single window, which was closed by a lattice or shutter of interlaced woodwork. Apparently, the shutter had not been properly secured or was too weak to bear his weight. As a result, he had fallen through and hurt himself badly.

Rather than seek God for help, Ahaziah sent his servants to inquire of a demonic entity called Baalzebub (lord of flies) as to whether or not he would recover. On the way, these servants were intercepted by the prophet Elijah who expressed to them God's extreme displeasure with the king's adherence to the worship of Baal. Elijah gave them an ominous prophecy, *"Now, therefore thus saith the Lord, Thou shalt not come down from that bed on which thou art gone up, but shalt surely die."*1 Because of his unconscionable evil, God was about to enact the removal of King Ahaziah. Elijah gave this ominous word and departed.

Ahaziah Ordered a Company of Soldiers to Kill Elijah

The servants of Ahaziah immediately returned with this dark word for the king. When asked, they described the prophet as a *"hairy man with a leather girdle about his loins."*2 With this information, the king instantly knew it was Elijah and became enraged. He then ordered a captain with a company of fifty soldiers to apprehend the prophet and (most likely) execute him on the spot.

The soldiers found Elijah waiting, sitting on top of a dusty hill, generally thought to be Carmel. His earlier mental depression had been healed by God's loving protection and kindness. What remained in the soul of Elijah was the pure essence of a warrior and defender of the faith. Now, he was back, as God's mighty prophet of fire, waiting for the threat that was sure to come.

Thus, King Ahaziah's captain and his fifty soldiers arrayed themselves at the bottom of the hill and shouted up at Elijah, *"thou man of God, the king hath said, Come down."*3 In using the term *"man of God,"* the captain was making fun of Elijah as if he were only a mere pretender. To order Elijah to surrender to the king was an insult to God. It can be described as a situation where the servant of an earthly king is ordering the servant of the King of the universe to obey his king. This rash action was a stupid mistake on the part of Ahaziah and a deadly error for the captain and his men. If Elijah submitted himself to them, because of Ahaziah's order, it would mean Ahaziah was a more powerful king than Almighty God.

The Lord Does Not Acquit the Wicked

Of course, all of this put the king and his soldiers in direct conflict with God. They were blinded by the demons they worshiped and foolishly crossed the trip wires of God. The Lord does not sit at His ease when dealing with enemies. He takes action. The Bible states, *"... the Lord takes vengeance on His adversaries and keeps wrath for His enemies."*4 God reserves *wrath* for His enemies. This is strong language for the faint of heart. While the Lord is slow to anger and ready to forgive, He will by no means acquit the wicked. When men are fueled by demons, they are "the wicked." Thus, what Elijah did next was a "vindication" of God's honor which had been challenged by the wicked in the land of Jezebel.

The Fire of God Exploded on the Soldiers

In response to the captain, Elijah, still seated, looked down from atop the hill and calmly asked God to vouch for him: *"If I be a man of God, then let fire come down from heaven, and consume thee and thy fifty."*5 Then, the fire of God instantly exploded and turned them to ash, floating in the mountain breeze.

Indeed, God would not have destroyed all of these men had there not been a sufficient cause to justify the act. It was certainly not done to assuage Elijah. Instead, God led the prophet to *confront* the evil standing below. The confrontation was Elijah's part. The rest was up to God.

Knowing the Mind of God is a Prophetic Mystery

Elijah *knew* how God wanted to handle things and merely announced this to the soldiers. Knowing the mind of God is a powerful weapon and a great mystery of the Lord's prophetic realm. It makes demons tremble. Also, Elijah's words were not a curse, but a *prophetic declaration* on behalf of Almighty God to establish the truth of His sovereign power.

Eventually, dark reports of this disaster reached the ears of the sickly king.

Sadly, this only served to anger the wicked king even more. In his rage, he cared nothing for the lives of these men that were sacrificed so foolishly. Of course, it is possible that his fierce anger was aggravated by his hopeless infirmity. Nonetheless, stupidity can be terminal and Ahaziah was drowning in it. Therefore, the enraged king ordered a second captain with a company of fifty soldiers to seize Elijah.

The Second Company of Soldiers

It is possible that this fresh company of men arrived at the bottom of Elijah's hill with something to prove. The captain was even more insolent than the first captain, commanding the prophet to *"Come down quickly"*6 and not waste his time dallying back and forth. This arrogance was likely the sense of the whole company. Tragically, they completely ignored the fate of the first company and the logical conclusion that any subsequent attempts to capture and kill Elijah would not end well.

The Fire of God Exploded Again

So, Elijah simply replies, *"If I be a man of God, let fire come down from heaven, and consume thee and thy fifty."*7 Again, the fire of God exploded on them, turning them into blackened ash. When this word reached the royal palace, the king reached for his migraine medicine and ordered another company of fifty to capture Elijah. Only the devil's impudence could make a man so headstrong as to send a total of 102 men to face down one prophet and then, after losing them all to fiery deaths, insist upon sending yet a third captain and company of fifty to Elijah's hill. But, that is exactly what Ahaziah did.

King Ahaziah Sent a Third Company of Soldiers

However, this time the captain was a different kind of man from the first two. This captain did not arrogantly stand below Elijah and shout up at him to quickly trot down and obey the king. This third captain did not want to die in falling fire, so he humbly "went up" and came before Elijah and fell on his knees in front of the prophet. The captain begged Elijah, *"O man of God, I pray thee, let my life and the life of these fifty thy servants, be precious in thy sight. Behold, there came fire down from heaven, and burnt up the two captains of the former fifties with their fifties: therefore let my life now be precious in thy sight."*8

An Angelic Being Speaks to Elijah

At that moment, the angel of the Lord said to Elijah, *"Go down with him: be not afraid of him."*9 Thus, Elijah got up and went with the captain to see the king. It is unknown whether or not Elijah was placed in restraints or left alone for this journey.

So, Elijah presented himself to the injured Ahaziah. The record does not reveal any real discourse between the two men, except for the words of Elijah: *"Thus saith the Lord, Forasmuch as thou hast sent messengers to inquire of Baalzebub the god of Ekron, is it not because there is no God in Israel to inquire of his word! Therefore thou shalt not come down off that bed on which thou art gone up, but shalt surely die."*10 So Ahaziah died according to the word of the Lord which Elijah had spoken. Thus, King Ahaziah was *removed* and this portion of Bible history was closed. Yet, hidden beneath the surface of this account is a wellspring of prophetic revelation that has relevance to American believers in the coming days.

God's Supernatural Rule of Three

The Word of God has unveiled a supernatural trichotomy or rule that revolves around the number three. This "Rule of Three" symbolizes wholeness and integrity. It represents power. Thus, the Word of God is revealed to mankind in *three* distinct dimensions. In this, Jesus, the living Word of God, is revealed in *person, principles* and *power.* It represents a spiritual transformation in believers beyond the initial work or sense of God's grace that might be termed *finishing* grace or even, great grace (more on this later). The Bible declares, *"And with great power gave the apostles witness of the resurrection of the Lord Jesus: and great grace was upon them all."*11 We need great grace for what lies ahead in America!

Three also represents great strength. The Scriptures declare, *"A threefold cord is not quickly broken."*12 We can find the strength of "three" dimensions woven throughout the Word of God.

God is manifested in *three* persons: *Father, Son* and *Holy Spirit*.13 The angelic seraphim cry, *"Holy, holy, holy,"* around the throne of God.14 He is the *thrice* holy God. The Old Testament tabernacle described in the Book of Exodus and based on heaven's model, consisted of three dimensions: (1) *an Outer Court; (2) the Holy Place;* and (3) *the Holy of Holies.*

Next, man created in the image of God, functions in *three* dimensions of soul, spirit and body. The blessing of God was passed down to *three* named individuals: Abraham, Isaac and Jacob.15 The deliverance of God was demonstrated in the lives of *three* faithful followers: Shadrach, Meshach and Abednego.16 Jonah was in the belly of a whale for *three* days and lived to tell of it.17 Salvation is a *tripartite* (three-fold) doctrine – a Christian has been saved (justification), is being saved (sanctification) and will be saved (*glorification*).

The Son of God holds a *three-fold* office – Prophet, High Priest and King. In Bethlehem, the wise men presented the baby Jesus with *three* gifts: gold, frankincense and myrrh.18 Jesus overcame temptation by the devil *three* times.19 At His transfiguration, *three* disciples (Peter, James and John) were witnesses of *three* things that happened supernaturally when *three* individuals (Jesus, Moses and Elijah) came together: (1) the Mosaic Law was fulfilled; (2)

the words of the prophets were fulfilled; and (3) the Son of Man came powerfully and visibly into His kingdom.20 Jesus' ministry was *three* years in length. He was crucified at age thirty-*three*, at three o'clock in the afternoon and rose from the dead on the *third* day.21

We learned from the Apostle Paul of the existence of *three* heavenly realms.22 Satan, the prince of the power of the air,23 roams the second heaven, but God reigns in the *third* heaven. The kingdom of God has *three* components: righteousness, peace and joy.24 Wholeness and completion or fulfillment (rest) is achieved in *three* dimensions of grace: (1) saving; (2) sanctifying; and (3) finishing.

John the Revelator saw *three* angels fly in the midst of heaven: (1) the first tells all the earth to worship God; (2) the second declares the fall of Babylon; and (3) the *third* angel declares that anyone who receives the Mark of the Beast (enemies) will receive God's wrath.25 There are more examples, but this should suffice to make the point.

Further, these things are not just fun facts from the Bible. Knowledge is power. Thus, there is tremendous power in store for those who have ears to hear.

The Rule of Three in Elijah's Ministry

When Elijah first burst onto the scene in the royal court of Ahab and Jezebel, there were *three* points of truth revealed: (1) Jehovah is the true God, not Baal; (2) Jehovah is alive, not dead; and (3) Jehovah controls nature, not Baal.

Elijah relied on supernatural sustenance *three* times in his ministry: (1) wild ravens fed him; (2) a widow fed him; and (3) an angel fed him.

When Elijah performed the miracle of raising the dead child, he stretched himself over the child's body *three* times. Then, the child came back to life.

In the cave on Mount Horeb (Sinai), Elijah was confronted by the power of God in *three* elemental displays: (1) wind; (2) earthquake; and (3) fire.

Interestingly, after the displays of wind, earthquake and fire at Horeb, God spoke to Elijah in a still, small voice. In this, the Lord gave a *three*-part assignment to Elijah: (1) anoint Hazael in Damascus to be king over Syria; (2) anoint Jehu to be king over Israel; and (3) anoint Elisha to be the next prophet after Elijah.

But there is more to this.

The three-part assignment to terminate Baalism also had *three* promised conclusions: (1) those who escaped the sword of Hazael would be killed by Jehu; (2) those who escaped the sword of Jehu would be killed by Elisha; and (3) seven thousand loyalists (to Jehovah) would remain after the purge.

Elijah was to anoint Hazael, Jehu and Elisha as *weapons of war* against Baalism in the land. In a prophetic sense, they represented the *three* furious elements of God's display on Horeb of wind, earthquake and fire. Their assignments were to utterly annihilate the evil followers of Baal.

Then, there were *three* confrontations with enemy soldiers at Mount Carmel. In two of them, the soldiers were burned to a crisp by the fire of God, but in the *third* event, Elijah did not call down the fire. Instead, at the prompting of an angelic being, Elijah was assured of his own safety and went with the captain to visit Ahaziah. Once there, Elijah repeated his prophecy that Ahaziah would indeed die because of his failure to serve Jehovah. The *third* confrontation became *grace* to both the final company of soldiers (who were not burned alive) and the king (who was given a chance to repent before his final breath, though scripture does not reveal that he did). Thus, the *third* confrontation brought forth the fulfillment of Elijah's prophecy of Ahaziah's death. It became a *"finishing."*

Jesus Made His Own Whip to Drive Out Evil Men

The *Elijah Awakening* will transform ordinary people into supernatural confronters. Why? It is because the prize will not go to the ordinary or the average. The power of the kingdom of God is only available to those who are willing to struggle for it.

Observe Jesus, the living epitome of confrontation.

Jesus never encouraged cowardice among His followers. They were awestruck when He drove the money changers out of the temple with a whip. In fact, Christ actually made the whip Himself prior to attacking these men and overturning their tables.26 It is time for the MAGA movement to begin making whips like Jesus.

Jesus confronted ambiguity and indecision. He drew a line in the sand and asked the willing to boldly step across it.27 He had good reason. The miracle dimension He walked in can only be attained by those who refuse to be driven away by vain philosophies and false promises of victory without voracity and vitality. There are no gray areas. The choice is black or white. People must choose this day whether to serve God or sell their souls to the Jezebel Agenda

Americans Need to Wrestle for the Blessing

Believers need to wrestle for the blessing as did Jacob who stubbornly said, *"I won't let you go until you bless me!"*28 We can possess the supernatural power of God to defeat the Jezebel Agenda in America. Today, Jesus is saying to America, *"If you want the power and glory of God in your lives, you must manifest a spiritual violence down to the depths of your souls. You must take the possibilities of the kingdom of God by the force of your faith. Move forward in My Name."*

Jesus' Purpose was to Destroy Evil Works

Today, many embrace the message of Jesus' love, but not His purpose. Jesus had a powerful purpose. The Bible declares, *"...for this purpose was the Son of God manifested, that He might destroy the works of the devil."*29 His purpose ought to be our purpose. We must manifest Christ to destroy the works of Satan in America. However, in this day of rioting, looting and violence in the streets, some cannot imagine themselves as fighters. Some look into their spiritual mirrors and visualize the elegantly attired bride of Christ. They cannot fathom wearing fatigues and combat boots. Such things are offensive to the religious sensibilities of some people. They have dressed for a wedding party, not a bloody battle. When they read about the Apostle Paul saying, *"...war a good warfare,"*30 some squirm and hope he was not referring to them. Frankly, most would rather not look evil in the eye when it is standing right in front of us.

Confrontation brings us into close proximity with the enemy. It requires a face to face approach. When Moses began his mission to rescue Israel from Egyptian bondage, he confronted Pharoah. Moses came face to face with the most powerful leader in the known world and spoke the Word of the Lord to him. When David walked out onto the battlefield to confront Goliath, he stood face to face with an enemy giant and knocked him flat by throwing a rock guided by angels. When Jesus was led by the Spirit into the wilderness, He confronted the devil. Jesus looked Satan right in the eye and said, *"Get thee hence, Satan..."*31

When Christ was crucified, He confronted Calvary's cross. He came face to face with His destiny. Jesus confronted every thought of failure and every whispering spirit that sought to keep Him out of the will of the Father. He confronted the cross for the joy of the kingdom that was set before Him. Confrontation leads the way to victory and it follows the footsteps of purpose.

From generation to generation, God has raised up people who will believe Him against all odds. He has called them to manifest Christ and destroy the works of the devil in supernatural confrontation. The hope of the church rests on nothing less than the bloody conflict of Calvary's cross and the willingness of our God to confront the wages of sin with the sacrifice of His own Son.

God Did Not Grant America's Title to Satan

We are created in the image and likeness of God. We are quickened and raised up and made to sit with Him in heavenly places. We shall not be defeated and we must never quit. The kingdom of God welcomes the passionate and the purposeful. Indeed the violent will take it by the force of supernatural confrontation. American believers will take back what the kingdom of darkness has stolen from us. The enemy has no right to take it and keep it. God did not grant America's title deed to the kingdom of darkness.

Consider the following.

When someone buys a car, their name is put on the legal title. Suppose a thief steals this car from the grocery store parking lot and drives it away. The thief may momentarily be in possession of the car, but the car title remains in the name of the legal owner. An act of theft does not transfer the auto's title to the thief. Stealing a car does not transform a crook into the rightful owner. Stealing the car only makes him a criminal. It does not matter if the thief brags to his associates of his "ownership" or sits on the car's hood for cute photographs to pass around. That which distinguishes true ownership is the lawful name on the title.

Stealing an election does not transform thieves into lawful office holders. Such people are nothing more than criminals. The act of stealing makes a thief an *enemy of God.* The Lord reserves wrath for such people. They shall reap the whirlwind.

Trump was God's Best Choice for President

Millions believe God put the name of Donald J. Trump on the title to the nation's highest office. From the heavenly throne, God extended His scepter and chose Donald J. Trump to be President of the United States of America for this period in our history. If this assumption is correct, God's choice was usurped or interrupted by enemies in the kingdom of darkness. Jesus declared, "*Truly, truly, I say to you, he who does not enter the sheepfold by the door but climbs in by another way, that man is a thief and a robber.*"32 Thieves always climb in by another way.

But American patriot believers will take back all that was allegedly stolen from us!

"Pursue: You Will Overtake Them and Recover All"

In 1 Samuel, Chapter 30, the enemy Amalekites came against David and his men who were away from the city at Ziklag. They *"climbed in by another way"*32 and abducted wives, daughters and sons and carried them away. David and his men arrived too late to stop them and this caused great distress among them. In fact, they were so distressed, they blamed David and wanted to stone him. So, David prayed and asked God, *"Shall I pursue after this troop? Shall I overtake them?"*33 God gave David the answer for all the ages. The Lord said, *"Pursue: for thou shalt surely overtake them, and without fail recover all."*33 The Bible records that when they obeyed God and pursued the enemy, *"there was nothing lacking to them, neither small nor great, neither spoil, nor any thing that they had taken to them: David recovered all."*34

The prophetic message to American believers right now is one of great urgency. God is saying, *"Pursue and you will overtake them. Then, without fail, you will recover all."* We must pursue the enemy to overtake him. Then, we will take back what he has stolen from the people of God. Without fail, we will recover all.

Three Confrontations and the Tectonic Political Shift

Out of many, there will be three decisive confrontations in the supernatural realm involving the *Elijah Awakening* in warfare with the kingdom of darkness. Two of these confrontations will result in the "fire of God" falling. The first fire will confirm that the God of Abraham, Isaac and Jacob is the true God of America and not Baal. The second fire will destroy the enemy's strongholds in key areas in America. Believers should closely monitor the state forensic election audits in the coming days and weeks. Heavenly truth will be soon be revealed in spite of demonic opposition and God has already arrayed the angelic host in preparation for these events. Finally, the third pivotal confrontation will trigger a *"removal of Ahaziah,"* which is a cleansing effect, causing a tectonic political shift in the nation back to the MAGA, America First agenda of "Trumpism" and a reaffirmation of America's love and support for the nation of Israel. MAGA patriot believers will cheer in the streets of America for they will *know* without doubt that God fights evil for them!

The message to the kingdom of darkness and its followers: Repent and turn away from wickedness. Justice is coming and time is short. A sea change is coming to America, orchestrated by God Himself and nothing can stop Him.

CHAPTER TEN

Parting the Waters

ELIJAH MIRACLE 8

"Elijah took his mantle, and rolled it up, and struck the waters; and they were divided here and there, so that they both went over on dry ground." 2 Kings 2:8 KJV

A merican "Elijahs" will soon roll up the mantle of the prophet and strike the waters in America to help set things in order. Since early 2020, American citizens have been on an incredible roller coaster ride through many troubles, toils and snares. From tyrannical lockdowns, caused by a suspicious viral pandemic, to election irregularities, that shoehorned pretenders into the White House, American patriots have been jammed through the wringer.

Believers should not worry.

Quite often, God sends His people into wilderness places to strip them of worldly illusions and fleshly limitations. This process always causes pain and suffering, because it is a spiritual boot camp for warriors. It is the only way we will ever see the power from on high. We have to walk the hard road to prepare us for hard won victories.

Jesus walked a hard road in the land of Moriah on His way to Calvary's cross. He suffered a nightmarish and bloody death. He was buried in a borrowed tomb. But, thank God, on the third day, He walked out of His own grave! Americans should take heart because it is not over yet. In fact, those of us who love God need to get ready to do the impossible. A great spiritual awakening is coming to our shores and God is about to move every mountain out of our way. Not even wild rivers will stop our progress.

You Can Run but You Cannot Hide from God

At this point in our Elijah journey, Ahab, Jezebel and Ahaziah have all died (as prophesied by Elijah). Ahaziah died from injuries sustained from falling out of his own window. Ahab was wounded in battle against the Arameans at Ramoth Gilead and bled out on the floor of his own chariot. Later, dogs licked his blood. Jezebel was hurled to the street from a high window by her own eunuchs and feral dogs devoured her. Alas, you can run, but you cannot hide from Almighty God.

After these events, Elijah and his servant Elisha, covered much ground together and Elisha gained valuable insight from time spent with the great prophet. He had hoped to learn even more. However, in Gilgal, God suddenly informed Elijah that his ministry on earth was finished and that he would be taken to heaven. God told Elijah to proceed across the Jordan River to a certain place where a heavenly chariot would translate him to glory. This was an unbelievable exit strategy, but quite fitting for the famed prophet of fire.

Elijah's Final Visits to the Schools of the Prophets

As Elijah pondered his last day on earth, he decided to visit the towns of Bethel and Jericho to inspect the schools of the prophets at both locations. These schools were founded as nurseries for the religion of Jehovah and as checks against the evil of Baalism. Elijah likely wanted to give them one last exhortation and blessing. He also attempted to convince Elisha to remain at Gigal, but the younger man steadfastly refused saying, *"As the Lord liveth,* *and as thy soul liveth, I will not leave thee."*1 So, with Elisha at his side, Elijah set off on a last journey.

The Bethel Visit

When they arrived at Bethel, the sons of the prophets (students at the school) came to Elisha and pointedly inquired of him as to whether he was aware that *"the Lord will take away your master today?"*2 Out of respect or fear, the students kept their distance from Elijah, because he was standoffish and absorbed in deep thought about the incredible revelation that was about to become reality to him. So, they approached Elisha with their curiosities. Elisha gave a curt reply, *"Yea, I know it; hold ye your peace."*2 After a time, Elijah came near to Elisha and attempted to talk him into staying at Bethel while he went on to Jericho. Elisha again refused saying, *"As the Lord liveth, and as thy soul liveth, I will not leave thee."*3 So, the pair went on their way to Jericho.

The Jericho Visit

Again, the same scenario played out. Students came out to press Elisha for his knowledge of the departure of Elijah and he hastily dismissed them. Again, Elijah came to Elisha and tried to persuade him to remain behind at Jericho while he went on to the Jordan crossing. Again, Elisha stood his ground and refused to stay, impressing upon Elijah that he would not leave him. So, the two of them went together down to the river.

It was at the river that things got interesting.

Fifty Witnesses at the River Miracle

The Bible records that fifty men of the sons of the prophets trailed along with the two and stood "afar off" to watch as Elijah and Elisha stood at the river's edge. Some have theorized that these students were curious as to how the two prophets would get across the river at a point where there was no ford. It is also likely they were aware of the miraculous history of this particular river, such as when the waters were parted by God for the Ark of the Covenant.4 It is also contemplated that these fifty students wanted to catch a glimpse of Elijah's departure and be witnesses of the event.

In today's crumbling America, many appear to be satisfied with standing "afar off" to watch things unfold. If our forefathers had chosen this methodology, we would still be under English rule. Instead, they rose up and broke free of the tyranny of the British crown. We need to roll up our sleeves and get ready to make a supernatural river crossing. Victory awaits just over, on the other side.

The Waters are Parted by God

Elijah and Elisha stood together on the bank of the river. All other human contact was left far behind. The prophet of the past and the prophet of the next generation, were together, with nobody to disturb them or separate them. The Jordan rolled its muddy waters past the two men, an obvious barrier to further advance. But they were not to be stopped. Jordan would be crossed and Elijah would soon ascend.

The Bible declares, *"And Elijah took his mantle, and wrapped it together, and smote the waters, and they were divided hither and thither, so that they two went over on dry ground."*5 The prophet rolled up his mantle and wielded it like the rod of Moses, smacking the surface of the waters, causing them to rise up into two liquid walls on either side of a miraculous pathway that was heretofore *invisible* to the earthly eye. But God's supernatural pathway was there, just the same. His pathway is always there. Thus, Elijah and Elisha walked across on *dry ground*. God's footsteps became their footsteps and the dry riverbed before them was as holy ground.

Now watch this.

The Supernatural Order of God

For a number of years, God and Elijah enjoyed a powerful relationship. With all of his faults and failures, Elijah loved the Lord and fiercely defended the faith. For reasons of God's choosing, Elijah walked in a supernatural existence. He went where God said to go. He said what God wanted said. Let the chips fall where they may. Even when Elijah panicked in fear of Jezebel's threat and hid in the wilderness, God protected him and encouraged him and pulled him together again. God kept Elijah in the fight against Baal. He worked awesome miracles through Elijah.

However, Elijah's miracles did not happen because Elijah possessed super powers. *He was a man just like us.*6 The miracles happened because Elijah walked in the supernatural order of God. This was the thing that separated Elijah from everybody else. He stepped where God told him to step. God walked him right up to the dark face of the enemy and the power exploded.

When we walk in the supernatural order of God, He fights the battle and the power explodes!

There is virtue in this.

The Supernatural Pathway

The writer of Proverbs said, *"In all thy ways acknowledge Him, and He shall direct thy paths."*7 So, there is a pathway that is directed by God. This pathway must be walked or stepped on. The Psalmist declared, *"The steps of a good man are ordered by the Lord."*8 Elijah's steps were ordered by the Lord. He walked on a supernatural pathway. This is a secret sauce for miracles.

The Bible says that the "good man" has ordered steps. To step into order, we must submit to the "good man" in us. This is an act borne of Spirit, not of flesh. From this, we can derive doctrine.

There is more.

The Bible says, *"... there is none good but one, that is, God..."*9 Fallen humans cannot be "good." So, God was manifested in the flesh (He became a man) and His name was Jesus. Jesus Christ is the Redeemer throughout the Old and New Testaments. Elijah and the Old Testament saints were aware of the promised Redeemer, and they were saved by faith in that Savior, the same way people are saved today.

The writer of Proverbs said, *"A good man obtaineth favor of the Lord..."*10 God spoke from heaven to express His favor of Jesus saying, *"This is my beloved Son in whom I am well pleased."*11 No other man in Scripture has ever been set apart in such a manner. Christ Jesus walks in the favor of His Father. Therefore, Jesus, the Redeemer, is "the good man."

The Steps of the Son are Ordered by the Father

Jesus observed what His Father did in heaven and that became the template for what He did on the earth.12 Thus, the steps of the Son are ordered by the Father. This order is revealed within a portion of the Lord's Prayer: *"Thy kingdom come. Thy will be done on earth as it is in heaven."*13 First, it is done in heaven, then on the earth. Jesus knows how to reach into the invisible kingdom of God and draw down into the earthly realm whatever He needs.

Jesus knows which way to walk. This explains why we must follow Him and not the other way around. His feet walk on water. His steps take us unharmed through lions' dens and fiery furnaces and angry mobs. His footsteps transport us beyond the temptations of Satan. We can follow Him through the valley of the shadow of death and fear no evil. In Christ, we live and move and have our being.14 His steps become our steps. When we can no longer walk, He will carry us. His footsteps become as ours. We cannot lose because when God is for us, nothing can stand against us. All things are possible!

God Calls Chaotic Waters to Order

Because of this, the waters *have no choice but to part* when God's path directs us right up to the river's edge. The river is not an obstacle for God. The river recognizes the Creator of all things and obeys His command to come into order. When the mantle of an "Elijah anointing" is brought down upon them, the waters divide. They surrender to the power of God and come to order. The Apostle Paul declared, *"Let all things be done... in order."*15

There is more.

God calls chaotic waters into order for the purpose of solving problems or creating opportunities for His people. On the second day of creation, God parted the waters to create the heavens and a place for the stars to shine. When the Egyptian army chased the Israelites across the countryside, they were forced to a halt at the Red Sea. So, God parted the waters of the Red Sea and the entire nation hurried across on dry ground. The waters fell on the Egyptians and drowned them, but not God's people. God's people always walk across on dry ground.

When Joshua came to the Jordan River with the priests and the Ark of the Covenant, God parted the river when their feet touched the water and the nation walked across on dry ground. When God parted the waters for Elijah and

Elisha, both men walked across on dry ground. Later, God parted the waters for Elisha and he walked across on dry ground, alone. God can bring things to order for one man or an entire nation.

God calls those things that be not, as though they were, to produce supernatural order. He directs us right up to the river's edge. Then, the waters part when Elijah smacks them with his mantle. The *Elijah Awakening* will soon impart this mantle to American believers and to God be the glory.

The natural state of wild rivers is chaos. They swirl in eddies and muddy pools. They roar in rapids, across the land and cut through solid rock, clawing their way to the sea. Rivers roll where they will. But, God calls rivers into order and makes the waters divide because He is the Creator of all things and He loves us.

Election fraud is like a wild river blocking our path to freedom.

When elections are stolen by criminals, bad things happen. The wrong people rise to power and take advantage. The demons rejoice from such activity. Chaos reigns. Good people are punished, freedom is lost and evil increases in the land.

Lunatics Claim Fraud Not Widespread Enough to Warrant Action

Despite the destruction that fraud can visit upon our democratic republic, the lunatic Left has continued to deny the existence of it in the 2020 elections. When they have been shown substantial evidence of wrongdoing, the corporate communists and their trained seals in the fake news media loudly dismiss the problem as "not widespread enough" to warrant action. This is absurd, but it has been our reality in America.

What if the Church suddenly declared that sin was not widespread enough to bother with? How would that play out? What if Elijah had sniffed, "It's not widespread enough to merit further action," when God told him to take a stand against Baalism. What if Jesus had decided the need to save lost mankind was not widespread enough and refused the cross?

Hosea declared, *"Then shall we know, if we follow on to know the Lord."*16 Americans need to *know* what happened. We need to know the next step. Then, we need to step where God steps. We have to *follow on* to know the Lord. Knowing the Lord is key to walking where He walks. We must *follow on* no matter what the fake news media says. No matter what the Marxist radicals say. No matter how many roadblocks they try to throw across our path. We will follow on!

Only the Word of God, illuminated by prophetic revelation, can provide adequate explanation and guidance for what is to come.

The Biden Regime and the Muddy River

The events that may have resulted in a Godless regime, squatting in the nation's capital, have worked to place a raging river right in front of us. American patriots have walked to the river's edge and watched the swirling waters rolling past. We have witnessed broken things floating past in those dark waters. Broken laws, lost jobs, mangled economic systems and constitutional freedoms have floated past. Pieces of our best lives have been swept away in the currents. The dark rulers of Baal have been momentarily appeased, causing a release of evil powers and lustful spirits from their thrones of iniquity over America. The skies have grown dark over America.

The Elijah Awakening and the Patriot Movement

However, the evil that has kidnapped America will not stand. God is about to make some changes because a remnant of true American believers (most are in the MAGA movement), are following the footsteps of God and He has heard our cries. Something huge is coming! The *Elijah Awakening* will soon help patriots who love God to roll up the prophet's mantle and strike the waters of chaos in America.

God Will Part the Waters in America

Then, the waters of the raging river will part, *hither and thither*, by the power of Almighty God. Those who know the ways and means of God will walk across on dry ground just like Elijah and Elisha. The truth shall set us free. When this happens, fake news and heathen political commentators will struggle to find words to describe it. They will scream and they will shake their fists with the rage of demons. Some, choosing to fight against truth with atheistic intellect, will lose their moorings in the blinding light of heavenly evidence exploding all around them.

But the waters will part just the same!

A Season of Rejoicing is Coming

In this exciting environment, God will again prove Himself to man. Faith will become substance. The evidence

THE ELIJAH AWAKENING

of things heretofore not seen will shatter every man-made myth. The Word of the Lord will come alive in supernatural proportions. We will enjoy a great season of rejoicing. Jesus said, *"But he that shall endure unto the end, the same shall be saved."*17 The river rolling past only marks the beginning. But, when we endure the race and God parts the waters, we shall be saved and strengthened to cross the finish line. We shall win the victory in the name of that "good man," Jesus!

America needs to take heart and praise the God of heaven. This too shall pass. It is not over until God says it is over. We need to get ready. God is about to part the waters of the roaring river and take us across on dry ground!

CHAPTER ELEVEN

A Chariot of Fire and the Whirlwind

ELIJAH MIRACLE 9

"And it came to pass, as they still went on,
and talked, that, behold, there appeared a
chariot of fire, and horses of fire, and parted
them both asunder; and Elijah went up by a
whirlwind into heaven." 2 Kings 2:11 KJV

To the horror of traitors, atheists, communists, election fraudsters, globalists, satanists, Baal worshipers and other DC swamp dwellers, a God-powered solution to the demonic assault on our nation is coming. As Elijah was delivered to heaven in a whirlwind with a chariot and horses of fire, the *Elijah Awakening* will explode across the heartland, in the fire of God. Already, there is a *"sound of* *marching in the tops of the mulberry trees."*1 God is taking the field in response to a deadly enemy arrayed against us!

When the whirlwinds of a genuine Holy Ghost revival blow across America, hearts will be changed. When hearts are changed, Jesus Christ is returned to His proper place as the object of all worship and glory. When God receives the glory that is due Him, He responds in a manifestation of supernatural power that destroys the works of the devil.

The coming revival will present Christ in power as few have seen Him because it will destroy the works of the kingdom of darkness that is crippling the nation. Therefore, America will be great again when the American church becomes supernatural again. Big changes are on the way. Indeed, the sound of the rushing mighty wind is already stirring.2

Mounting Evidence of 2020 Election Fraud

Meanwhile, God is getting ready to anoint His "Elijahs" with miracle power to confront Baalism in America. As of this writing, the forensic election audits are progressing regardless of wild-eyed, fake news, "on-air" meltdowns to spin it all away as right-wing conspiracy theories. In spite of leftists fighting the process like wildcats, loud calls for forensic audits are metastasizing into other battleground states across the country. Hard evidence seems to be mounting that the 2020 election was stolen by corrupt criminals being controlled by the enemies of America, foreign and domestic. Dark predictions have been made that a soiled Biden regime will try to weaponize its own DOJ to attack these audits to shut them down and hide the truth from the American people. However, while the lawless Left trots out the next disinformation campaign, God has other ideas.

The Bible declares, *"Even though bad people intended to harm us, God intended it for good to accomplish what is now being done, the saving of many lives."*3 God will send the whirlwind to actuate a "changing of the guard" in our nation. When this occurs, fake news media types, like caged simians, will screech and hurl themselves at the bars of their cages. Those who understand the deep things of God will rejoice for the possibilities presented in that hour.

The Changing of the Guard from Elijah to Elisha

With fifty sons of the prophets watching them from afar, Elijah and Elisha crossed over the Jordan River on dry ground. Elijah turned to the younger man and said, *"Ask what I shall do for thee, before I be taken away from thee."*4 And Elisha responded, *"I pray thee, let a double portion of thy spirit be upon me."*4 Elijah scratched his chin thoughtfully and said, *"Thou hast asked a hard thing: nevertheless, if thou see me when I am taken from thee, it shall be so unto thee; but if not, it shall not be so."*5

Rather than, *"Thou hast asked a hard thing,"* the literal translation of Elijah's comment is, *"Thou hast been hard in asking."* The term "hard" should be read as: *"bold."* Elijah gave the younger man a great compliment. In this, he was saying that Elisha was "bold" in his request for something so big *only God* could give it. There is a great lesson in this for all of us – if you want big, *ask big.*

The Bible declares, *"... ye have not, because ye ask not."*6 Jesus said, *"... if two of you shall agree on earth as touching any thing they shall ask, it shall be done for them of my Father which is in heaven."*7 There are millions in America who love the Lord. It is time for us to agree together (as touching any thing– as if it was already possessed and in hand) that God will soon deliver our nation from the powers of darkness and the Jezebel Agenda.

The Chariot and Horses of Fire and the Whirlwind

So, Elijah and Elisha continued walking along when suddenly, there appeared *"a chariot of fire, and horses of fire, and parted them both asunder; and Elijah went up by a whirlwind into heaven. And Elisha saw it, and he cried, My father,* *my father, the chariot of Israel, and the horsemen thereof. And he saw him no more: and he took hold of his own clothes, and rent them in two pieces. He took up also the mantle of Elijah that fell from him, and went back, and stood by the bank of Jordan.*8

Elisha picked up Elijah's mantle that had fallen to the ground and stood on the bank of the Jordan River. Then, he took the mantle and struck the waters saying, *"Where is the Lord God of Elijah?"*9 Incredibly, the waters rolled back again and Elisha walked across on the dry riverbed.

A large delegation of the "sons of the prophets," watching from afar, came near to Elisha. They proclaimed, *"The spirit of Elijah doth rest on Elisha."* and bowed to the ground before him.10 It is unknown as to whether or not this bunch actually saw Elijah taken up. They immediately began casting doubt on Elijah's translation into heaven by offering theories that the prophet may have been simply relocated on a mountain or in a valley. They urged Elisha to send out a search party to find Elijah. The prophet refused at first, then reluctantly acceded to their wishes after being worn down by their relentless prodding. So, they sent fifty men to waste three days fruitlessly searching. Indeed, Elijah had departed in a blaze of glory.

Chariots of Fire and God's War Angels

The "chariot of fire" speaks to the angelic forces of heaven. David affirmed this truth saying, *"The chariots of God are tens of thousands and thousands of thousands; the Lord is among them..."*11 The angels are God's messengers, *"sent forth to minister for them who shall be heirs of salvation."*12 Zechariah saw chariots with horses of various colors. They were described by an angel as the four spirits of the heavens sent by God according to their color into the north and south.13 These are war spirits (angels) and they represent God's judgments on wickedness in the world. His truth is relentless. Even though evil may be purged from the church, God's war angels will hunt it down no matter where it tries to hide.

Horses and chariots are used in the Bible as emblems of power and glory associated with mighty conquerors. God uses them to crush His enemies and save His people. Habakkuk declared, *"Thou didst ride upon thine horses and thy chariots of salvation."*14 Isaiah spoke of the coming of the Lord *"with his chariots like a whirlwind."*15

After the time of Elijah, and later in Bible history, the servant of Elisha was filled with fear at the sight of a large assemblage of Syrian soldiers with horses and chariots. Elisha simply asked God to open his servant's eyes allowing him to see beyond the veil of the natural realm. Then, the young man saw the mountain *"full of horses and chariots of fire round about Elisha."*16 Elisha told his servant, *"Fear not: for they that be with us are more than they that be with them."*17 When God is for us, nothing can stand against us. The angelic warriors of God wield flaming swords and cause rulers of darkness to tremble.

The Explosion of Revival Fire and the Prophecy of Joel

The host of heaven, on horses and chariots of fire, are coming to deliver America from the enemy's grip. We are rapidly approaching a tipping point in America where revival fire will explode on us in a sovereign move of God. This event will not be man-made or man-controlled, but something else entirely. It will be like wildfire.

It will be *"that which was spoken of by the prophet Joel."*18 The prophet Joel saw an end-time event when the Spirit of God is poured out upon all flesh causing sons and daughters to prophesy, and young men to see visions, and old men to dream dreams. In that explosion of heavenly power, God will pour out His Spirit on men and women alike and they will prophesy.18

In the Book of Acts, the Apostle Peter appropriated the Old Testament prophecy of Joel to explain what happened to the 120 believers gathered together in the upper room of a house on the Day of Pentecost. Following Peter's lead, we can utilize Joel's prophecy to explain in spiritual terms what is about to happen in America. Out of this phenomenon, will come the *Elijah Awakening* whereby men and women will be called of God as "Elijahs" to prophesy and demonstrate the power of God in America. They will *rise up* in the force of the whirlwind of God to help deliver the nation from evil.

The Spiritual Reformation of America and God's Landing Zones

The coming whirlwind explosion of Holy Ghost power in America will be more properly termed a "spiritual reformation," and it will not be neat. It will be messy. Explosions tear things to pieces. Some things are torn apart and others are rearranged by the blast. During the Vietnam war, the US military used an explosive "detonating cord" that looked like nylon cord to move the jungle out of the way to make landing zones for helicopters. An entire tree line would be transformed into stumps all at once in the blast. Then, large bulldozers could move in and clear the area.

What God is about to do in America could be compared to jungle clearing and landing zone building in Vietnam. In this, God is getting ready to build many Holy Ghost landing zones for His purposes in America. Indeed, the Armies of God will soon be awakened in a heavenly whirlwind.

The Whirlwind of God

Elijah *went up* by a whirlwind into heaven. God would simply not allow His prophet to be slaughtered by the psychotic Jezebel and her wicked assassins. In like manner, God protected the integrity of Elijah's ministry all the way to its awe-inspiring conclusion. God confirmed His word through the miracles of Elijah. Therefore, as Elijah gave himself so faithfully to honor God, the Lord returned the favor by taking him straight up to glory in the heavenly kingdom. It was the deliverance of God manifested in a whirlwind.

God often uses whirlwinds and chariots of fire to prove His power and majesty. The Bible declares, *"The Lord is slow to anger, and great in power, and will not at all acquit the wicked: the Lord hath his way in the whirlwind and in the storm, and the clouds are the dust of his feet."*19 Isaiah wrote, *"... the Lord will come with fire, and with his chariots like a whirlwind, to render his anger with fury, and his rebuke with* *flames of fire.*"20 These scriptures paint a strong picture of an Almighty God who will not compromise with evil. They present a God who has been pushed into a fury.

God is Provoked to Rage by Evil Leaders

Throughout the Bible, God is most often provoked to rage when humans reject Him to worship and consort with entities from the kingdom of darkness. This wicked activity, more than any other, was the reason God set His face against Ahab, Jezebel, Ahaziah and others documented in the Bible. They all worshiped Baal, Asherah and Molech and thus, were neck-deep in sexual perversity and child sacrifice. In their capacities as rulers, they led God's people into idolatry, blasphemy and abomination. As a result, God was provoked to rage and each of these individuals paid a horrible price for their evil actions.

What about the globalist blight on American thinking? Is God provoked to anger by the hidden poison of ancient Baalism permeating America's culture? Has God softened His approach to perversity, child sacrifice and blasphemy?

The Arch of Baal in Washington, DC

In September of 2018, a reconstruction of the ancient Arch of Baal of Palmyra, Syria, was set up for several days on the Capitol Mall in Washington, DC to celebrate global cultural heritage, according to the Institute for Digital Archaeology.21 It was reported therein that the Arch, which stood some 65 ft. tall, was built in the third century by Septimus Severus and linked the city's central colonnaded street to its main temple, the temple of Baal. An ancient pagan religious leader would pass under the arch on his way into the Temple of Baal to frolic with temple prostitutes and walk under it again on the way out.

It was reported that some people were quite taken with the Arch and its placement against the columns of the Capitol as if they were seeing through the eyes of the ancients. Seeing through the eyes of the ancients indeed! Jezebel would have been ecstatic about this display. It was also reported that the original Arch of Palmyra in Syria was reduced to rubble by ISIS in 2015. The Arch was also displayed in New York City with great fanfare.

Why was this architectural reminder of Jezebel's evil religion of child sacrifice and sexual deviance erected within sight of the Capitol?

Woke White House Cancels God from National Day of Prayer

On May 6, 2021, the "woke" Biden White House issued a National Day of Prayer proclamation without *once* mentioning God or Jesus Christ. This was outrageous! Why would Joe Biden, an alleged Catholic, omit or cancel Almighty God from the National Day of Prayer? What deity did Biden intend for Americans to pray to? Was Biden ashamed of invoking the name of Jesus? The Apostle Paul declared, *"For I am not ashamed of the gospel, because it is the power of God that brings salvation to everyone who believes…"*22

America was founded as a Christian nation. The Bible says, *"Blessed is the nation whose God is the Lord."*23 George Washington once remarked, *"It is impossible to rightly govern the world without God and the Bible."* The founders knew that Christianity provided the moral values and intellectual foundation for a stable and prosperous nation. These truths are the reason that America succeeded and thrived. But now, ravenous jackals controlled by *"spiritual wickedness in high places"*24 have infiltrated every nook and cranny of our national government.

The Enemies of God and the Sword of Jesus

The time for mincing words is over. American believers are at war with the kingdom of darkness for the soul of our nation. Americans who love God, stand on one side of the conflict. The forces of Satan are arrayed on the other. Americans will either stand for God or war against Him. There is nothing complicated about this. Any person or political party aligned with the Jezebel Agenda, Baal and/or the dark kingdom are the enemies of God. Period.

Consider the war-like words of Jesus: *"Think not that I come to send peace on earth: I came not to send peace, but a sword."*25 The sword is an instrument of war and death. Jesus did not mean that He came to create discord among humans. He is the Prince of Peace. However, Jesus is saying that *"the sword"* is one of the *effects* of the gospel of Christ. Its mighty power will slice through and separate devils from believers. Alas, it is wickedness, not the gospel, that causes hostility between humans. But, Jesus came to put a sword through the heart of darkness.

Indeed, God's truth marches with us to the very end.

Jesus said, *"And this gospel of kingdom shall be preached in all the world for a witness unto all nations; and then shall the end come."*26 In this, Jesus was responding to the question of his followers: *"What shall be the sign of thy coming,* *and of the end of the world?"*27 Many confuse the answer to this question with certain characteristics of the end-time. Jesus spoke of wars, famines, pestilences, earthquakes, persecutions, false prophets and the loss of love among the very elect. While these are the characteristics of the end of an age, they are not sign of the end-time.

Characteristics versus Signs of the End-Time

Characteristics put the emphasis on negative events of the natural realm – dangers, toils and snares – things that adversely affect the saints. We are seeing these things today. Indeed, unless we stop them, they will only get worse.

Signs put the emphasis on supernatural demonstrations that identify the saints of God. Jesus said, *"And these signs shall follow them that believe; In my name shall they cast out devils; they shall speak with new tongues; They shall take up serpents; and if they drink any deadly thing, it shall not hurt them; they shall lay hands on the sick, and they shall recover."*28 Indeed, signs identified the newly minted apostles. The Bible documents that after Jesus ascended into heaven, these individuals *"went forth and preached everywhere, the Lord working with them, and confirming the word with signs following."*29

The Church is God's Agency on Earth for Waging War against Satan

Jesus has indicated that the Gospel will be preached *for a witness*. When Elijah called down the fire of God on the altar, the explosion of fire was a witness to the authenticity of Jehovah as the true God. There can be no witness among lost humans, blinded by lies, without the demonstration of God's power – the only true sign – in the earth. Literally, the "shock and awe" of God will produce faith and separate the wheat from the chaff and precious from vile. This is how the church is revived and brought into the spiritual order of God. The church is God's mechanism or agency *on the earth* for waging war against the kingdom of darkness.

Therefore, the church must be reformed and refreshed in order to carry on, just like Elisha took up the sacred mantle and carried on after Elijah.

In our Elijah story, the Bible records the sudden appearance of the chariot and horses of fire to Elijah and Elisha which separated them. Then, Elijah went up by the whirlwind. God separated the old generation from the new. He made a distinction between the former and the latter. The latter generation (Elisha) would have a double portion of Elijah's spirit.

A New Elijah Generation will Arise to Fight

We are about to witness the *Elijah Awakening* in America, in the great revival that is to come. In that hour, a double portion of the Elijah spirit or anointing will rest upon a new generation to take up the prophet's mantle to fight against the spiritual wickedness that is now destroying our beautiful America. We cannot falter in our supernatural assignment to stand against the demonic lies of Baalism and the Jezebel Agenda.

To all patriots who love the Lord: Take heart and look to the Eastern skies and listen with spiritual ears. You will hear the rumbling of thousands of heavenly chariots and horses of fire. You will feel the winds of God on your face, already blowing across the land. The Elijah anointing will return in the whirlwind of God to confront evil in America.

*"Fear not, stand still, and see the salvation of the Lord..."*30

CHAPTER TWELVE

Killing Jezebel

"And he said, This is the word of the Lord, which he spake by his servant Elijah the Tishbite, saying, In the portion of Jezreel shall dogs eat the flesh of Jezebel: And the carcass of Jezebel shall be as dung upon the face of the field in the portion of Jezreel; so that they shall not say, This is Jezebel." 2 Kings 9:36 KJV

Dark agendas, like invading armies, cannot move forward to conquer without a source of supply. To destroy an evil agenda that emanates from a supernatural entity seated on a throne in the kingdom of darkness, you must attack its power source or supply lines. If the monster cannot eat, it will pack up and leave. Dark rulers release their evil power into nations when they are appeased (fed) through the wicked acts of human followers. To defeat and unseat a dark ruler, its source of supply (evil acts seen as "worship" by the entity) must be destroyed with the power of the Gospel.

In ancient Israel, the source of supply for Baalism was "worship" that included sexual perversity and child sacrifice. Baalism became a nation-devouring, spiritual monster and its chief architect and advocate was the evil Queen Jezebel. Under her seductive spell, King Ahab, "... *reared up an altar for Baal in the house [temple] of Baal, which he had built in Samaria.*"1 Baalism became the *national religion,* usurping the worship of Jehovah.

It was a disaster to marry Jezebel. After Ahab became the King of Israel, the Princess Jezebel of Tyre (Phoenicia) was brought to the northern kingdom to be his bride. This marriage would establish a trade and military alliance whereby Israel would be partners with the wealthy and powerful pagans of Phoenicia. However, God had commanded that Israelites should not marry outside of the nation of Israel. Moreover, Israelite kings were forbidden from marrying foreign princesses for political alliances. The Bible says, *"For the lips of a strange woman drop as an honeycomb, and her mouth is smoother than oil: But her end is bitter as wormwood, sharp as a two edged sword. Her feet go down to death; her steps take hold on hell.*"2

Jezebel Bewitched Ahab and Plunged Israel into Evil

Jezebel quickly bewitched Ahab and brought him to heel. The pair then proceeded to provoke God to a boiling rage by subverting the worship of Jehovah and plunging Israel deeply into the demonic religion of Baal and its horrors. No extremity of wickedness was beyond the imaginations of Jezebel.

Jezebel and the Execution of Prophets

Like all followers of Baal, she painted her face and dressed immodestly to encourage an environment of sexual indulgence. Worship rituals included sexual acts aided by temple prostitutes. Bestiality was also practiced. It was the lure of sexual indulgence that made the blasphemy of Baalism so palatable to the people. Efforts to promote the restrictive ways of Jehovah were thus ignored. To gain further compliance and control of the masses, wicked Jezebel murdered nearly all of the prophets of Jehovah and threatened the life of Elijah, vowing to kill him.

No evil act was considered "out of bounds."

Ahab began to covet a certain vineyard next to the royal palace. So, Jezebel engineered a false charge of blasphemy against Naboth, the vineyard owner, which sealed his fate – execution. This murderous scheme allowed King Ahab to seize the coveted vineyard for his own. However, these crimes did not escape the attention of Almighty God. They never do. As a result, Ahab and Jezebel were cursed to die by the prophet Elijah, according to the Word of the Lord.3

The Road to Perdition in America

The Jezebel Agenda helped pave the road to perdition in America (see Chapter 1) and radical, God-hating, leftist Democrats became purveyors of the doctrines of devils. The Covid "plandemic" changed everything for them. It may have allowed crooked operatives to hornswoggle a presidential election with millions of questionable mail-in ballots, no voter ID, no signature verification, ballot harvesting and ballots counted days after the election was over. With fangs bared behind N-95 masks, they brazenly imposed a Marxist, totalitarian regime, utilizing practices favored by the Chinese Communist Party. In this, the "elites" (business, media, academic and entertainment) came together in a demonic effort to obliterate America's democratic form of government and undermine the very foundations of our country. Such efforts produced the need for an Ahab-like "pretender" at the helm.

Consider the clueless Joe Biden.

Biden and the Chimp

It has been contemplated that a blindfolded chimpanzee hurling a dart at a page of stock listings could do as well, if not better, than a professional manager. Simply replace the stock listings with a list of presidential tasks, swap out the professional manager for Biden and let the ape commence throwing darts at a leftist wish list pinned to the wall. It is likely the chimp would enjoy higher poll numbers than Sleepy Joe, with less napping, groping and sniffing.

The spectacle of Biden's calamitous presidency reduced to rubble all around him is excruciating. During his first days of defiling the White House, Biden, like a drunken tyrant, willfully dragged America into the abyss with a slew of outrageous executive orders, memorandums, proposals and proclamations. These included actions that: threw open the southern border, ended the Keystone XL pipeline; abolished the 1776 Commission; rejoined the Paris Climate Accord; re-engaged with the WHO; revoked orders that excluded illegal aliens from US Census; ended sexual orientation and gender identity discrimination; lifted restrictions on abortion funding and many more. Biden has demanded a more aggressive level of control over the nation's K-12 classrooms with "Critical Race Theory," an evil replacement for history using identity politics and a warped view of American civics and institutions.

More insanity will surely follow and the king appears naked and oblivious to it all.

A Reckoning is Coming for Marxist Radicals and Others

However, evil labeled as "the great reset," "social reform" and "transformation" will eventually be revealed for what it is. The truth will out because God said so. The Bible declares, *"For there is nothing covered, that shall not be revealed; neither hid, that shall not be known."*4 Marxist revolutionaries, liberal lunatics, fake news media, traitors, race baiters, Green New Deal crazies, gun grabbers, election fraudsters, Baal worshipers, foreign and domestic, should beware. Soon, a reckoning for their sins will be visited upon them.

Consider King Ahab.

King Ahab's fate was sealed by the murder of Naboth to steal his vineyard. God instructed Elijah to confront Ahab in the vineyard of Naboth and prophesy that God would deal with him by ending his life and cutting off all his descendants: *"In the place where dogs licked the blood of Naboth shall dogs lick thy blood, even thine."*5 When Ahab heard this, he tore his clothes, put on sackcloth and fasted and crept about meekly. In response to Ahab's repentance, God was merciful and postponed the destruction of Ahab's dynasty until after Ahab was dead.6

The Killing of Ahab

In time, Elijah's powerful prophecy came true. God used Ahab's own false prophets to entice him into join-ing the battle at Ramoth-Gilead, where he was shot with a "random" arrow through the joints of his armour. A coat of mail covered only the breast, to somewhere near the last rib; and below this it had an appendage (skirts) consisting of movable joints. Between this appendage and the coat of mail there was a groove through which the arrow passed and entered Ahab's lungs or abdomen and thereby, inflicted the mortal wound that killed him. He laid on the floor of his own chariot and bled to death by sunset. Later, they "… *washed the chariot in the pool of Samaria* [where the temple prostitutes bathed]; *and the dogs licked up his blood… according to the word of the Lord.*"7 So, the kingdom was turned to Ahaziah, the son of Ahab and Jezebel.

The Sons of Ahab and Jezebel

Elijah prophesied of Ahaziah's death. Then, Ahaziah died from injuries sustained from falling out of his own window – he was purged by God. Thus, the kingdom was turned to another son of Ahab and Jezebel named Jehoram. His death would come at the hands of a man of war named Jehu.

Earlier in the history of Elijah, when the prophet was hiding in a cave at Mount Horeb, God passed by in a great wind, earthquake and fire and then, spoke to Elijah in a still, small voice. God gave certain and explicit instructions to Elijah (see Chapter 9). Among them, were three appointments that included: Hazael to be king over Syria; Elisha to be the next prophet; and a man named Jehu, the son of Nimshi, to be anointed as king over Israel.

Jehu the Executioner of God

Before his reign as king, Jehu was a commander in the army of Ahab. The Jewish historian, Josephus, believed that Jehu rode side by side with another officer behind Ahab in his chariot. The Bible reveals that Jehu was actually the son of Jehoshaphat, although he is more commonly mentioned as the son of Nimshi, his grandfather, perhaps because Nimshi was more well-known. Jehu's name means, "Yahweh is he." It was his God-given task to annihilate the house of Ahab, along with the worship of Baal.

After he was anointed to be king, Jehu began plotting a rebellion against King Jehoram. The king had gone to Jezreel to recover from wounds received in a previous battle. Jehu ordered his men to cordon the city of Jezreel to entrap King Jehoram within its limits and to keep Jehu's anointing a secret from him. Then, Jehu and his men approached Jezreel in chariots until they were spied by a watchman.8 They halted just outside the city.

The Killing of Ahab's Son and Grandson

After sending out two riders to make inquiries as to Jehu's purpose, King Jehoram and King Ahaziah (Ahab's grandson from Judah) rode out to meet him, each in his own chariot. Ironically, they came together on land formerly owned by Naboth. When Jehoram realized Jehu's deadly intentions, he turned to flee and was shot to death (through his back) by Jehu's arrow. Ahaziah was also shot when he tried to escape by running through a nearby garden house. Ahaziah managed to travel to Meggido before he collapsed and died.9

Jezebel was next.

The Killing of Jezebel

Jehu drove his chariot to the palace in Jezreel, where he found Jezebel watching him at her window. The Bible documents that Jezebel had already been informed of Jehu's violent appearance at Jezreel and prepared herself for his arrival at the palace. She carefully arranged her hair. The Bible records that she painted her face – literally meaning "her eyes" – whereby, she stained the eyelids with a black powder created from pulverizing antimony, or lead ore, mixed with oil and applied with a small brush on the border, to increase the luster of the eye. Jezebel did not do this to seduce Jehu with her charms, but to put him in a state of awe by her imposing and royal appearance. She desired to die as a queen. When she was ready, she stationed herself at a high window to watch.

When Jehu rolled up within earshot, Jezebel taunted him saying, *"Had Zimri peace, who slew his master?"*10 Put in simpler language, this meant, *"Can a traitor or anyone who rises against his superior succeed?"*11 In this, Jezebel taunted Jehu as a "traitor" to highlight her belief that Jehu had cursed himself by murdering his own king.

Jehu steadfastly ignored Jezebel's words and shouted up at the window, *"Who is on my side? Who?"*12 Then, two or three eunuchs (chamberlains or royal household managers) peered at Jehu out of side windows. Jehu shouted at them, *"Throw her down."*12 So, upon Jehu's command, the eunuchs surrounded Jezebel and forcibly, hurled the proud queen out of the window.

Some have contemplated that as she fought them, she screamed with such vigor the walls shook. Thus, her defenestration was as violent as her treatment of Jehovah's prophets. Upon its violent contact with the ground below, her body burst so that some of her blood was thrown against the wall. Then, Jehu moved his horses over her and trampled her down, driving over her with his horses and chariot.12

With that done, Jehu immediately took possession of the palace and set about to appease his great hunger. Interestingly, not only the eunuchs of Jezebel, but the royal household servants were ready to serve him, for the queen-mother was hardly dead before Jehu was seated at a banquet. In all of his eating and drinking, Jehu had forgotten about his victim in the street. Suddenly, he remembered that even vile Jezebel was of a royal rank. Some believe he may have experienced remorse in his mandate for her burial: *"Go, see now this cursed woman, and bury her: for she is a king's daughter."*13 However, Jehu was not concerned that Jezebel was the wife of a king or mother of a king. Rather, his only concern what that she was the daughter of a king. For Jehu to purposely deny her a proper burial would have been regarded as an unpardonable insult by the reigning Sidonian monarch and cause trouble.

Feral Dogs Devoured Jezebel

The bloody body of Jezebel had been left on display in the street. As Elijah had prophesied, the feral dogs devoured her like ravening wolves. A decade after the death of the feckless Ahab, all that remained of Jezebel was her skull, the feet and the palms of her hands. When Jehu's men reported this fact to Jehu, he restated the prophecy of Elijah saying that, *"In the portion of Jezreel, shall dogs eat the flesh of Jezebel."*14 He went on to add that Jezebel's end was so dehumanizing that she was rendered unrecognizable.

The Sword of Jehu Eradicated Baalism in Israel

Jehu annihilated all who were in alliance with King Ahab and Jezebel, as God had commanded (through the prophet Elijah). He put the sword to all the evil priests of Baal and destroyed the temple of Baal, thus eradicating Baal worship in Israel.15 The Bible documents this result saying, "*Thus Jehu destroyed Baal out of Israel.*"16 God blessed Jehu for his obedience, giving him a dynasty that would last to the fourth generation.17

The violent execution of Jezebel was the culmination of several years of God-directed efforts to eradicate Baalism in Israel. Powerful evil forces, natural and supernatural, were necessarily confronted and defeated in this ancient drama. Based on these events, it is evident that the rulers of darkness involved in that battle did not easily give up their territories and go quietly into the night. A *spiritual warfare process* was required to win the day. In Israel, the process began with the fiery confrontations, prophecies and prayers of the prophet, Elijah. It was finalized in the violence of the man of war, Jehu.

Military Structure of the Kingdom of Darkness

The *Elijah Awakening* will soon become a declaration of war on the kingdom of darkness that grips America. The enemy forces are led by Satan (Lucifer was an angel of the cherub order)18 and the fallen angels that rebelled against God long ago in the dateless past.19 The evil kingdom, likely patterned after God's heavenly kingdom, has a military structure formed in hierarchies. The Apostle Paul explains: *"For we wrestle not against flesh and blood, but against principalities, against powers, against the rulers of the darkness of this world, against spiritual wickedness in high places."*20

Vine's Dictionary states: "The context of Ephesians 6:12 (*"not against flesh and blood"*) shows that not earthly potentates are indicated, but spirit powers; who, in consequence of human sin, exercise satanic and therefore antagonistic authority over the world in its present condition of spiritual darkness and alienation from God."

Principalities are the Highest Rank

Under the command of Satan, Paul listed *principalities* as those who hold the highest positions of rank and authority. From the original Greek word *arche,* the term speaks to princes and chief rulers of the kingdom of darkness; they are first in rank or power and constitute a high order of evil spirits. They have likely held their positions since the fall of Lucifer.

Powers are Evil Angelic Beings

Next, Paul placed emphasis on a second-tiered group of evil beings called *powers,* from the Greek noun *exousia.* This speaks to evil angelic beings who possess delegated authority or influence. These entities receive their marching orders from first-tiered principalities.

Rulers of Darkness and Spiritual Wickedness in High Places

In the third-tier, *rulers of the darkness of this world* are the administrators of evil concentrated on regions or cities. This term *kosmokrator* speaks to ruling over the worldly affairs of human beings – government and politics. Beneath them in the fourth-tier, Paul lists entities called *spiritual wickedness in high places.* The term *epouranios* speaks to demons or unclean spirits that are sent forth to afflict humanity with widespread viciousness, chaos and malevolence.

The kingdom of darkness advances through CONTROL using *manipulation, intimidation* and *domination.* A brief overview of its battle strategy is presented in four stages that are also contained within the Jezebel Agenda:

THE ELIJAH AWAKENING

1. Control cultural atmosphere with cancel culture by limiting liberty and religious freedom through conversations and mindsets (Jezebel Agenda).
2. Control social climate though appetites, actions and desires of the inhabitants of a territory (Jezebel Agenda).
3. Control a territory (create a stronghold) by dividing the inhabitants according to economic, racial, cultural and social differences (Jezebel Agenda).
4. Control the inhabitants of the territory by demonic oppression and possession (Jezebel Agenda).

The Kingdom of God is Superior to Satan's Forces

America is under heavy assault at the time of this writing. The battlefield of human minds has been ravaged. What we are witnessing in America is a corollary of the events taking place in the supernatural realm. The dark kingdom controls geographic areas by controlling the minds of human beings with deceptions and lies, keeping them trapped in a lost condition.

However, when the Gospel is advanced deeper and deeper into enemy territory, Satan loses control. This loss of satanic territory is accomplished when human minds are wrested from his control and turned to Christ. Elijah

225

accomplished these goals with fasting, prayer, prophetic confrontation and the display of signs and wonders confirming the Word of the Lord.

The forces of Almighty God include the armies of heaven and the earthly Army of God (human believers). There are millions of us. We must advance and attack the kingdom of darkness in Spirit and in Truth, fighting for the souls of humans who are lost and perishing without the saving knowledge of the Gospel. Indeed, Satan has blinded many in America to the truth. Therefore, it is incumbent on us to deliver and demonstrate the Gospel to set lost Americans free, thereby destroying the works of the dark kingdom.21

Now watch this.

Spiritual Warfare on Principalities and Dark Rulers

Direct confrontation with principalities and high rulers of darkness is probably above the pay grade of most Christians. However, the Apostle Paul declared that Christians are called to wrestle against the evil influences of these upper-level entities in the heavenlies. He stated that the weapons of our warfare are mighty through God to the pulling down of strongholds. We can engage in warfare against these dark rulers by directing our prayers and petitions *about them* to God Almighty. Then, God will respond with an appropriate level of power to rectify the need.22

However, Jesus and the apostles did speak directly to lesser powers (unclean spirits) that had possessed a person. Those entities were cast out when they were commanded by the name and authority of Jesus Christ to leave their victim. Sometimes, the demons were particularly stubborn in the eviction process and stronger measures were needed. Jesus knew this and explained, "... *this kind does not go out except by prayer and fasting.* "23 Fasting moves the believer into great faith in God, which moves God. Then, God snaps His fingers and demons run screaming into the ozone.

However, what our Lord and the apostles did in casting out these demons is not the same as attempting to directly confront Satan's upper hierarchies of principalities and rulers of the kingdom of darkness. Herein lies America's great spiritual problem and the prophetic mission of this book. Where Elijah dealt with this level of satanic oppression in Israel, we must now deal with it in America, or lose the country to a hellish lunacy.

Daniel's Model for Supernatural Warfare with Rulers of Darkness

The model for this level of supernatural warfare was presented by Daniel, a visionary of the apocalypse, survivor of the lions' den and called *"prophet,"* by Jesus Himself.24

In a time of great trouble, caused by an unseen, supernatural enemy, Daniel sought God's help for his people in Jerusalem. He fasted and prayed for 21 days. Daniel stated, *"In those days, I Daniel was mourning three full weeks. I ate no pleasant bread, neither came flesh nor wine in my mouth, neither did I anoint myself at all, till three whole weeks were fulfilled."*25

In response to Daniels' prayer, one of God's high-ranking angelic beings appeared. The men with Daniel could not see it, but they heard the angel's voice and fled the scene in abject terror, *"...and the voice of his words were like the voice of a multitude... but a great quaking fell upon them, so that they fled to hide themselves."*26

However, Daniel saw the angel which appeared as a man clothed in linen. His waist was wrapped with fine gold. The Bible records the angel's face was bright like lightning and his arms and feet like highly polished bronze. This sight caused Daniel to faint.

Interestingly, John the Revelator saw a similar angelic being that cried out with a voice like the roar of a lion.27 Ezekiel saw angels of the cherub order that had the face of a lion. Jesus is the Lion from the tribe of Judah. These things are not for the faint of heart.

The angel gently roused Daniel and helped him into an all-fours, kneeling position, braced on the palms of his hands. Then he told Daniel to rise to his feet and spoke to him, *"Fear not, Daniel: for from the first day that thou didst set thine heart to understand and to chasten thyself before thy God, thy words were heard, and I am come for thy words."*28

The angel explained that the "Prince of Persia" [a principality in the kingdom of darkness] had obstructed him for 21 days, requiring Michael, one of God's archangels, to come help him break through to complete his assignment.29 Perhaps no other verse in the Bible speaks more clearly than this description of the invisible dark rulers that are set over nations.

God Sends the War Angels

The angel clearly told Daniel that he came because of Daniel's prayers. This is proof positive that God responds to the prayers of His people and sends His angels to help us. Next, it proves the importance of prayer combined with fasting. If Daniel had not continued with prayer and fasting together for the whole 21 day time period, the angel would not have been able to break through the enemy lines. Indeed, there is a direct relationship between the actions of believers and how God decides to move on a city or a nation. This has nothing to do with earning God's favor. Fasting and prayer, in this instance, has everything to do with moving us into agreement with the will of God and into spiritual order. Satan is to chaos, as God is to order.

After the heavenly battle, the angel of God pulled back the veil in the supernatural realm to allow Daniel to catch a glimpse of the satanic forces arrayed over the natural authority structures of the nations of the earth. In other words, this demonic ruler, set as a "Prince of Persia," was exerting his dark influence over the region of ancient Persia (Iran) and its human prince (or king), to produce evil in the land to destroy the souls of humans. This same dark activity is happening right now over America. Even weather patterns are affected by these evil "princes of the air."

Daniel did his part in securing the defeat of this demonic prince of Persia by agreeing with God in prayer and fasting. To this end, Michael, one of God's "chief princes" (a high ranking commander of heaven's angelic forces) was sent to ensure victory. Together, these mighty war angels of God defeated Satan's dark ruler.

Unexplained reports of so-called "UFOs" in the American skies are increasing. Many will attribute such sightings to "alien activity," without realizing they may be catching glimpses of angelic beings flashing through the heavens, in preparation for what is to come next. We should rejoice at these signs! They are proof that God is already sending His war angels to America.

Now watch this.

Daniel Did Not Pray Against Evil Territorial Entities

There is no Biblical record that Daniel prayed against demons, dark rulers or even *mention* such things in his prayer. He did state in prayer that *God* had brought upon Israel *"a great evil."*30 Daniel confessed the wickedness and rebellion of the people and asked God to turn away His anger from them. Moreover, it is important to recognize that Daniel did not know about the supernatural conflict in the heavenly realm prior to an angel informing him about it. Thus, the focus of Daniel's prayer was not *concentrated* on overcoming evil, supernatural entities.

What is the learning lesson here?

The Word of God never suggests that believers are to command high ranking fallen angelic rulers of darkness to give up their territories or anything else. In response to Daniel's fasting and prayer, God sent the powerful archangel Michael to deal with the fallen angels ruling over Persia and Greece. In fact, the content of the Gospel of Jesus Christ has an intrinsic *"power"* unto salvation, thus there is no need for believers to attempt "High Noon" duels with dark rulers.31 Thus, when we fast and pray to God, He will take the reins and deal with such high-level devils, as needed.

The Power of Jesus and the Army of God

Marvelously, Jesus Christ can easily overpower these dark principalities. His authority has been exerted or delegated to the earthly realm through human believers who agree with Him and persevere in the prayer of faith. Christ releases His mighty power in a partnership with His people when they are arrayed as the Army of God. We become soldiers in this supernatural army the moment we are anointed by the Holy Spirit and empowered with knowledge and discernment of the real conflict that is occurring in the invisible realm over America. Fasting and prayer strengthens our spiritual partnership with Jesus, our mighty King of Kings.

The events recorded in the Book of Daniel serve as a model of how the *Elijah Awakening* can actualize the will of God in America. The fasting and prayers of Daniel, that brought the angels of heaven to his aid, were no different than the fasting and prayers of Elijah, when he confronted Jezebel and Ahab and called down heavenly fire, to destroy Baalism and the works of Satan. Patriotic believers can use the same great strategy for defeating the Jezebel Agenda in America.

God is Ready to Make America Great Again

In this great awakening, the Holy Spirit will move on the hearts of individuals to rise up in fasting and prayer, as modern "Elijahs," in every state of the Union, using the prayer models of Elijah and Daniel to call forth the heavenly attack on the rulers of darkness that are seated on thrones of iniquity over their capital cities. With the unction of the Holy Spirit, American believers will also confront the wickedness of human rulers, just as Elijah confronted Ahab and Jezebel. The evil Jezebel spirit must be eradicated in our nation. In this way, things will change for the better in America.

We must prepare our hearts and minds, for the winds of God are already blowing. The revival of the *Third Day* is coming. The *Elijah Awakening* is coming. A great transformation of the Church is coming. A great spiritual harvest in America is coming. Big changes in our government are coming.

Indeed, God is more than ready to Make America Great Again because we will Make America God's Again!

AFTERWORD

In my past career, as a pastor and evangelist, I never claimed to be a prophet, but from time to time, God allowed me opportunities to peek into the prophetic realm. I know His voice, though it comes in gentle whispers and I have to strain to hear it. This is one of those times and it is why I know the subject matter of this book was God-breathed. Marvelously, I also know I'm not the only person God has entrusted with this message. Soon, other Spirit-filled, prophetic voices will come forth to confirm and verify the truth of what has been presented here. This is how the Lord does things in His Church.

During the Texas "deep freeze" in February of 2021, I was marooned in an RV in the Texas hill country. Roads became roller coasters, covered in snow, frozen and mostly impassible. Millions suffered as statewide power outages caused horrific shortages of heat, water and food. This event was a monument to the utter lack of preparation by those in charge. In the midst of those dark days, the Lord invaded my consciousness to remind me of a nation-shaking revival, He revealed to me some years ago. (Donald A. Moss, *The Third Day: A Revelation of the Coming Revival,* Writers Club Press 2002). Once the Lord had my attention, He proceeded to lay out His plans for a very unique calling of "Elijahs" within the coming revival. It was like Ezekiel's *"wheel in the middle of a wheel."*[1] Admittedly, it seemed like a fever dream at first, but then, things progressed and this book came into focus to deal with the spiritual war that must be mounted in the supernatural realm.

In the natural realm, the wonderful MAGA movement must continue its powerful progress to legally purge the Republican Party of globalist RINOs, weaklings and leftist sympathizers, conduct forensic audits in every state of the Union and so on. We must continue to "primary" every single politician who thinks the 2020 election was "fair" and "over with." MAGA, America First, candidates must present themselves and win and win and win! But these activities in the earthly realm are not what God wanted me to focus on. My assignment was to point American believers to the supernatural realm, the coming revival and the war on evil that must be declared by Christian believers.

Thus, the *Elijah Awakening* is focused primarily on spiritual warfare against the enemies of God and the invisible rulers of darkness that exist over America for the purpose of corrupting and manipulating human leaders. This explains the maniacal, abnormal activities that have transpired throughout 2020-2021 and will continue unabated until we stop them. Their nefarious goals include "globalism" and a "one-world" form of government in preparation for the terrible reign of the man of sin, the Antichrist.

Globalism has absolutely nothing to do with the things of God or the Great Commission of Jesus whereby we are commanded to *go ye into all the world, and preach the Gospel to every creature.*"2 We can effectively preach the Gospel to the world without "taking the mark" of the Party of Davos. America must remain a sovereign nation under God, as founded, with secure borders and the Rule of Law to govern our way of life. We must take care of America *first*, before we can take care of the rest of the world.

Here's the bottom line: Powers, principalities and rulers of darkness will not stop their America-destroying agenda without a fight and it's up to us (just like Elijah and Jehu) to call down the fire of God and throw them out of Jezebel's high window.

So, the *Elijah Awakening* will surely include confrontations in the natural realm, but this book outlines how God will use American believers, as "Elijahs," in warfare with spiritual wickedness in high places which speaks of the supernatural realm. The Lord is about to make some big changes in America that will push back evil and destroy the works of Satan. In His mercy, God desires to give America "space to repent" and get our house in order.

Therefore, we are on the threshold of the Promised Land and in the words of Caleb, *"… Let us go up at once, and possess it, for we are well able to overcome it."*3 In the words of the great patriot and honorable military veteran, Stephen K. Bannon, we need to take *"Action! Action! Action!"*

If I don't see you before then, I will see you on the other side.

God bless America.

God bless Texas.

Let us Make America God's Again.

Donald A. Moss

The Prayer of Elijah:

"Lord God of Abraham, Isaac, and of Israel, let it be known this day that thou art God in Israel, and that I am thy servant, and that I have done all these things at thy word. Hear me, O Lord, hear me, that this people may know that thou art the Lord God, and that thou hast turned their heart back again." (1 Kings 18:36-37 KJV).

NOTES

(Unless otherwise indicated, all scriptures are from the King James Version Bible.)

Introduction

1. Posted to Instagram, October 24, 2020
2. Erskine podcast, February 27, 2021
3. Revelation 12:9 NIV
4. Job 1:7
5. 1 Peter 5:8
6. Luke 10:18-19 NIV
7. Amos 5:19 NIV
8. Matthew 17:11
9. 2 Corinthians 3:17
10. Daniel 11:32

Chapter 1: The Jezebel Agenda

1. 2 Corinthians 3:17
2. Isaiah 5:20 NIV
3. Genesis 12:3
4. Psalm 33:12
5. Exodus 20:3
6. Ephesians 4:27
7. Psalm 94:20
8. 1 Kings 16:33
9. 1 Kings 18:19
10. Jeremiah 2:20 NIV
11. Jeremiah 2:24 NIV
12. Isaiah 57:5 Amplified Bible
13. 2 Kings 14:28; 17:18
14. Jeremiah 19:1-3; Lamentations 4:8-10
15. Leviticus 18:21
16. Luke 17:2
17. Matthew 12:30

Chapter 2: The Elijah Awakening

1. Matthew 17:11
2. 1 Kings 16:33
3. James 5:17 NIV

4. Amos 3:7
5. Ephesians 4:11
6. Revelation 2:29
7. Numbers 11:29
8. Jeremiah 1:7-10
9. Psalm 105:15
10. Luke 10:19

Chapter 3: Elijah Miracle 1 – The Drought

1. 1 Kings 17:1
2. Exodus 34:14 NIV
3. 1 Kings 18:21 NIV
4. Deuteronomy 11:16-17 NIV
5. Hebrews 9:4 NIV
6. 1 Samuel 4:4
7. Joshua 3:15-17
8. Exodus 25:13-15
9. Numbers 4:15
10. 2 Samuel 6:1-7
11. 1 Samuel 6:5
12. 1 Samuel 5:8-12
13. 1 Samuel 6:1-15
14. Jeremiah 12:17 NIV
15. Deuteronomy 11:11 NIV

16. John 14:12 NIV
17. John 19:30
18. Romans 4:17
19. Matthew 6:10
20. John 5:19
21. 1 Corinthians 2:16
22. Matthew 16:19
23. Proverbs 13:22

Chapter 4: Elijah Miracle 2 – The Ravens

1. 2 Corinthians 3:17
2. 1 Kings 17:3-4 NKJV
3. Genesis 8:6-7
4. Psalm 147:9 NIV
5. Luke 12:24 NIV
6. Leviticus 11:13 ESV
7. Matthew 6:11 NIV
8. 1 Kings 19:7
9. 1 Kings 17:4
10. 1 Kings 17:7
11. Luke 22:42
12. 1 Kings 17:8 NIV

Chapter 5: Elijah Miracle 3 – A Woman and the Endless Supply

1. Matthew 26:12-13 NIV
2. 1 Kings 17:9 NIV
3. 1 Kings 17:10-11 NIV
4. 1 Kings 17:12 NIV
5. 1 Kings 17:13 NIV
6. Luke 6:38
7. Proverbs 3:9
8. Matthew 6:33 NIV
9. Hebrews 11:1
10. Zechariah 4:6 NIV
11. 1 Kings 17:14 NIV

Chapter 6: Elijah Miracle 4 – Raising the Dead

1. Romans 8:22 NIV
2. John 12:24 NIV
3. Romans 6:11
4. 1 Corinthians 2:9-10 BSB
5. Matthew 4:4
6. 1 Kings 17:20 NIV
7. 1 Kings 17:21 NIV
8. 1 Kings 17:24 NIV

9. I Kings 17:17
10. Genesis 2:7
11. Psalm 146:4 ESV
12. 1 Kings 17:22 NET
13. 1 Kings 17:20
14. Psalm 122:6
15. Jeremiah 5:9 NIV
16. Matthew 11:12

Chapter 7: Elijah Miracle 5 – Calling Down Fire on the Altar

1. 1 Kings 18:1-2 NIV
2. 1 Kings 18:6-7
3. 1 Kings 18:17 NIV
4. 1 Kings 18:18 NIV
5. 1 Kings 18:19 NIV
6. 1 Kings 18: 21 NIV
7. 1 Kings 18:22-24 NIV
8. 1 Kings 18:27 NIV
9. 1 Kings 18:36-37 NIV
10. 1 Kings 18:39 NIV
11. 1 Kings 18:40 NIV
12. 1 Kings 19:1
13. Isaiah 14:13-14

14. Genesis 11:1-9 NIV
15. Matthew 6:24 NIV
16. Matthew 3:10-12 NIV
17. Hebrews 12:29 NIV
18. Luke 12:49 NIV
19. Acts 1:8

Chapter 8: Elijah Miracle 6 – Calling Down the Rain

1. Isaiah 44:3 NIV
2. Psalm 72:6
3. Isaiah 45:8
4. Ezekiel 34:26
5. Hosea 6:1-3
6. John 7:38 NIV
7. Matthew 12:43
8. 1 Kings 18:1
9. 1 Kings 18:42
10. 1 Kings 18:1
11. Matthew 14:14 NIV
12. Luke 6:12 NIV
13. Matthew 6:6 NIV
14. Philippians 3:13
15. Psalm 40:1 NIV
16. I Kings 18:43

17. 2 Kings 6:16
18. 1 Kings 18:44 NIV
19. 1 Kings 18:45-46
20. Acts 5:29
21. 1 Kings 19:1
22. 1 Kings 19:2 NIV
23. 1 Kings 19:3 NIV
24. Romans 11:17
25. Ecclesiastes 3:8

Chapter 9: Elijah Miracle 7 – Calling Down Fire on the Enemy

1. 2 Kings 1:4
2. 2 Kings 1:7
3. 2 Kings 1:9
4. Nahum 1:2 NIV
5. 2 Kings 1:10
6. 2 Kings 1:11
7. 2 Kings 1:12
8. 2 Kings 1:13-14
9. 2 Kings 1:15
10. 2 Kings 16-17
11. Acts 4:33
12. Ecclesiastes 4:12

13. Matthew 28:19
14. Isaiah 6:3
15. Deuteronomy 1:8
16. Daniel 3:28
17. Matthew 12:40
18. Matthew 2:11
19. Matthew 4:1-11
20. Mark 9:1-9
21. Acts 10:39-40
22. 2 Corinthians 12:2
23. Ephesians 2:1-2
24. Romans 14:17
25. Revelation 6:6-11
26. John 2:15
27. Mark 10:21
28. Genesis 32:26 (paraphrased)
29. 1 John 3:8
30. 1 Timothy 1:18
31. Matthew 4:10
32. John 10:1 ESV
33. 1 Samuel 30:8
34. 1 Samuel 30:19

Chapter 10: Elijah Miracle 8 – Parting the Waters

1. 2 Kings 2:2
2. 2 Kings 2:3
3. 2 Kings 2:4
4. Joshua 3:16
5. 2 Kings 2:8
6. James 5:17
7. Proverbs 3:6
8. Psalm 37:23
9. Matthew 19:17
10. Proverbs 12:2
11. Matthew 3:17
12. John 5:19
13. Matthew 6:10
14. Acts 17:28
15. 1 Corinthians 14:40
16. Hosea 6:3
17. Matthew 24:13

Chapter 11: Elijah Miracle 9 – A Chariot of Fire and the Whirlwind

1. 2 Samuel 5:24 (paraphrased)
2. Acts 2:2

3. Genesis 50:20 (paraphrased)

4. 2 Kings 2:9

5. 2 Kings 2:10

6. James 4:2

7. Matthew 18:19

8. 2 Kings 2:11-13

9. 2 Kings 2:14

10. 2 Kings 2:15

11. Psalm 68:17 (paraphrased)

12. Hebrews 1:14

13. Zechariah 6:1-8

14. Habakkuk 3:8

15. Isaiah 66:15

16. 2 Kings 6:17

17. 2 Kings 6:16

18. Joel 2:28-29; Acts 2:16-17

19. Nahum 1:3

20. Isaiah 66:15

21. digitalarchaeology.org.uk/washington-dc

22. Romans 1:16

23. Psalm 33:12

24. Ephesians 6:12

25. Matthew 10:34

26. Matthew 24:14

27. Matthew 24:3

28. Mark 16:17-18
29. Mark 16:19-20
30. Exodus 14:13

Chapter 12: Killing Jezebel

1. 1 Kings 16:32
2. Proverbs 5:3-5
3. 2 Kings 21:19,23
4. Luke 12:2
5. 1 Kings 21:19
6. 1 Kings 21:29
7. 1 Kings 22:38
8. 2 Kings 9:16-17
9. 2 Kings 9:18-27
10. 2 Kings 9:31
11. 1 Kings 16:10; 18-20
12. 2 Kings 9:32-33
13. 2 Kings 9:34
14. 2 Kings 9:36-37
15. 2 Kings 10:23-28
16. 2 Kings 10:28
17. 2 Kings 10:30
18. Ezekiel 28:14
19. Revelation 12:4

20. Ephesians 6:12
21. Romans 1:16
22. 2 Corinthians 10:3-6; Ephesians 6:11-18
23. Matthew 17:21 NKJV
24. Matthew 24:15
25. Daniel 10:2-3
26. Daniel 10:6-7
27. Revelation 10:3
28. Daniel 10:12
29. Daniel 10:13
30. Daniel 9:12
31. Romans 1:16

Afterword

1. Ezekiel 1:16
2. Mark 16:15
3. Numbers 13:30

Donald A. "Donnie" Moss is a grandfather, former pastor, evangelist, police chaplain and 4th generation Texan. Descended from German pioneers in the Texas hill country, his family was depicted by his cousin Janice Woods Windle in her saga of the Texas Revolution, *True Women* (directed by Karen Arthur, Craig Anderson Productions and Hallmark Entertainment, 1997), with Angelina Jolie, Dana Delaney and Annabeth Gish. From management positions with a major oil company to evangelizing violent street gangs, Moss has led an interesting life. Ordained to the ministry in 1990, he hosted Christian television and radio programs, founded a full-gospel church and traveled nationwide as an evangelist and gospel singer. In the early 2000's, working with an award-winning producer and crack team of musicians, ranging from Grand Ole Opry players to a member of George Strait's "Ace in the Hole Band," he wrote and recorded several songs which landed on country radio charts in America and in Europe. Moss is a graduate of the University of Houston/Clear Lake, Oklahoma Bible College and Seminary and also attended the prestigious South Texas College of Law. He is the author of several books, including *The Third Day: A Revelation of the Coming Revival* (Writers Club Press 2002).